THE BASICS

Tragedy: The Basics is an accessible and up-to-date introduction to dramatic tragedy. A comprehensive guide for anyone undertaking a study of the genre, it provides a chronological overview and history of tragic theory. Covering tragedy from the classics to the present day, it explains the contextual and theoretical issues which affect the interpretation of tragedy, examining popularly studied key plays in order to show historical change. Including a glossary of key terms and suggestions for further reading, *Tragedy: The Basics* is an ideal starting point for anyone studying tragedy in literature or theatre studies.

Sean McEvoy teaches English and Classical literature at Varndean Sixth Form College and the University of Cambridge, UK.

The Basics

TRAGEDY

THE BASICS

Sean McEvoy

Routledge
Taylor & Francis Group

LONDON AND NEW YORK

First published 2017
by Routledge
2 Park Square, Milton Park, Abingdon, Oxon OX14 4RN

and by Routledge
711 Third Avenue, New York, NY 10017

Routledge is an imprint of the Taylor & Francis Group, an informa business

British Library Cataloguing in Publication Data
A catalogue record for this book is available from the British Library

Library of Congress Cataloging in Publication Data
Names: McEvoy, Sean, 1959- author.
Title: Tragedy : the basics / by Sean McEvoy.
Description: Abingdon, Oxon ; New York, NY : Routledge, 2017. |
Series: The basics | Includes bibliographical references and index.
Identifiers: LCCN 2016020506| ISBN 9781138798908 (hardback : alk. paper) |
ISBN 9781138798915 (pbk. : alk. paper) | ISBN 9781315756349 (ebook)
Subjects: LCSH: Tragedy--Handbooks, manuals, etc. | Tragic, The. |
Tragedy--History and criticism--Theory, etc. | Drama--Technique. |
Drama--History and criticism.--Theory, etc.
Classification: LCC PN56.T68 M44 2017 | DDC 808.2/512--dc23
LC record available at https://lccn.loc.gov/2016020506

ISBN: 978-1-138-79890-8 (hbk)
ISBN: 978-1-138-79891-5 (pbk)
ISBN: 978-1-315-75634-9 (ebk)

Typeset in Bembo
by Saxon Graphics Ltd, Derby

CONTENTS

suffering in Western culture by writing tragedies for nearly 2,500 years. Hugh Grady offers a useful working definition of stage tragedies:

> They are plays that take on issues of death, of suffering, of identity, of human nature, of human meaning and more. They never supply tendentious answers to any of these issues but instead explore, curse, rage, joy and wonder in ways that shift as we move from culture to culture and age to age.
>
> (Grady 2014: 796)

In fact, as Grady suggests, what we call tragedy is constantly evolving, and the problem with the term is that once we start using it to describe one particular form of theatre the genre has already moved on to a related, but different kind of work (Grady 2014: 792).

Tragedy can be found in all art forms: in fiction, in poetry, in music, in dance, in opera, in the visual arts, in television drama, in graphic novels and probably in computer games. This book, however, is focused on theatrical tragedy, without denying for a moment the equal validity and importance of other kinds of art as specimens of the tragic. Tragedy began on the stage in ancient Greece, and this book will trace its development in the theatre from ancient Athens to the present day. The scope of this book is also limited to the theatre of Europe and America and the drama of the Western tradition. Again, this is not to dismiss or denigrate tragic art in other cultures in other traditions at different periods of history. Indeed, I hope that readers of this book may subsequently want go further, and to study tragedy as it appears in other art forms and in other parts of the world. But given the space available, this book is written for students of Western theatrical tragedy, which remains a central and much-studied strand of the genre.

Ancient Greek tragedy dramatises the relationship between the immortal gods and mortal humans in its attempt to make sense of death and suffering, injustice and cruelty. When dramatic tragedy was revived again Christianity offered a narrative which could be used to explain why these things happen, and will end for some, but it seems that narrative was never strong enough to stop dramatists feeling the need to explore their own societies and values through the medium of tragedy. When science and reason began to wield a powerful influence in Western thought, in a movement sometimes known as the **Enlightenment**, tragic suffering came to be seen by some as a part of a benevolent process leading ultimately to a better world. In the twentieth century the idea that history was working its way towards a happy ending for all lost a great deal of credibility for many, and some influential critics proclaimed the death of tragedy itself. But theatrical tragedy is still being written in the twenty-first century, and still has important things to say about our world today, as this book will show.

This book starts with the Greeks and Romans, and considers what tragedy meant in these two ancient, but still formative and influential cultures. In this chapter, and all the subsequent ones, there is an account of a number of representative (and often studied) plays of the period. There is also a brief account of the social, political and cultural context in which the plays were first written and produced. In between the plays you will also find shaded boxes which present the ideas of important theorists and critics who have written about tragedy. Generally speaking the content of the boxes relates directly to the texts in that chapter, but some – such as the ideas of Aristotle, Hegel and Nietzsche, who appear in Chapter One, have a wider relevance to the whole book. When references are made to other books the author of the book, date of publication and the page number referred to appear in brackets. References to plays in Chapters Two and Three often give act, scene and line numbers (e.g. 3.3.53–60) rather than page numbers; but, when it is helpful, the page number of the edition referred to appears at the beginning of the reference. Full details of the book referred to can be found in the References section at the back, listed alphabetically by author. Full reference is given the first time the text under discussion is mentioned; just the page numbers subsequently. Unless otherwise stated, all references to Shakespeare's plays come from *The Complete Works*, second edition, edited by Stanley Wells and Gary Taylor (Oxford: Oxford University Press, 2005). Important terms are explained in the glossary, and whenever terms listed in the glossary appear in the text they are in **bold type**.

A book on plays that present misery, suffering and death might seem a gloomy prospect. But not only does the genre of tragedy contain some of the most powerful and beautiful plays in world literature, it also offers a series of remarkable insights into how Western culture has sought to understand what is valuable in life, and even, in the words of the contemporary British tragedian Edward Bond, most valuably, to talk of both 'the causes of human suffering and the sources of human strength' (Bond 2013: 109).

1

GREEKS AND ROMANS

CLASSICAL TRAGEDY

CONTEXTS: THE FESTIVAL OF DIONYSUS AT ATHENS

Our word 'tragedy' comes from the ancient Greek word *tragoidia*. There's no agreement about the word's origins. It may have meant 'goat song' (Hall 2010: 1), perhaps referring to the ritual slaughter of an animal which accompanied the original performances. Sacrifice to the gods was always an important part of Greek public events, and for the Athenians the theatre was perhaps the most important of these.

All the ancient Greek plays which have survived were performed in Athens at the great annual festival in honour of the god Dionysus, who was the god of wine and drunkenness, but also of the theatre. There was a connection: at the theatre dancing, singing and acting produced an altered state of mind for performer and audience – and the performance itself was a religious ritual. The Athenian tragic theatre was a unique event, a sacred state celebration where the citizen audience became emotionally involved in the suffering of the characters but also explored religious, political and social issues as a community.

The first tragedies were performed in about 534 BCE when Athens was ruled by a small group of rich aristocratic families, but all the plays we have were written after the establishment of the democracy in 508/7 BCE. Athens was at that time the most powerful of the different city states of the Greek world. Its central democratic institutions were the Assembly and the law courts. The Assembly made law and decided questions of peace and war and consisted of the entire citizen body of the city (the *demos*), which in fact comprised less than 20 per cent of the city's population, since it did not include women or slaves. The large juries in the law courts were also drawn from the citizens. In both institutions the people sat on a semicircular slope around a central area where opposing parties argued their cases, then voted to express the opinion of the people on the issue. The Theatre of Dionysus, located on the southern slope of Athens' citadel, the Acropolis, had a similar layout to both the Assembly and the law courts, and at the end of three days of tragic performances the audience would also vote, in this case to decide which tragic dramatist had won the festival that year. The first tragedies were not then commercial entertainments which people could choose to attend if they wished to and could afford it. They were the centrepiece of a religious and civic event which was a crucial part of Athenian cultural and political life, and shared some common formal features with other democratic institutions. In all these institutions so much depended on the purposeful use of language and argument, and an anxiety about the power of language to persuade or to deceive is central to so many Greek tragedies.

The Festival of Dionysus took place in late February or early March. It drew visitors from all over the Greek world, but its main audience was the male Athenian citizen body. It looks as if women didn't attend; or, if some did, they would not have been the 'respectable' wives of those citizens. They took no part as writers or performers or otherwise (Goldhill 1997a: 61–6). During the festival there was an expectation for all citizens to attend the theatre. It cost two obols to get in, but the state provided a grant to any citizen who could not afford this sum. Some scholars believe that the fifth-century BCE theatre could hold up to 16,000 spectators (Goldhill 2004: 223); others that temporary wooden seating was erected for the Festival which could only accommodate 4,000–7,000 (Csapo 2007: 99). On the first day of the festival four rituals took place. First, animal sacrifices were supervised by the ten generals, the most important military and political officers of the state. Then a list of citizens who had benefited the city in the previous year was read out, and chests of silver bullion, the tribute of other Greek subject-cities, were paraded in the theatre. Finally, the state-fostered orphans of war veterans who had just come of age were presented with armour and weapons and took an oath of loyalty to the city and were given special seats. Each of these rituals set out to promote the power and prestige of the Athenian state and its democratic values. Hymns to Dionysus sung by boys' and men's choirs called dithyrambs completed the first day. Yet, even though Athens was proud of its theatre, the plays that followed on subsequent days did not set out particularly to glorify the city (though at times they did that), but rather to question and contest the community's values and ideals: they sought to encourage 'self-reflection on personal, familial, intellectual and political issues of general concern' (Goldhill 2004: 232). The earliest tragedies, then, set out to provide a communal exploration of the most serious issues; it is no surprise that death and suffering should be at their heart.

Normally, on the second day of the Festival, five comedies were performed, and a jury selected the best play. Then on each of the following three days three tragedies by a single author were performed, followed by a 'satyr play': a short comedy featuring a chorus of satyrs, half-man half-goat creatures with large erect phalluses (Wiles 2000: 31). At the end of day five another vote took place to determine which tragic poet had triumphed that year.

Three professional actors played all the speaking roles. The performance area was known as the orchestra, a circular (or, in this period possibly trapezoidal) 'dancing floor'. The actors shared this space with the chorus. The chorus consisted of young amateurs, originally twelve in number, later fifteen. Readers and audiences today, used to modern dramatic forms, can overlook how central the chorus were to the Greek theatre. The tragic chorus were on stage for all but the opening lines of the play, participating in the action and also singing and dancing five 'odes', which punctuated but also commented on the 'episodes' of the play. Principally, they helped the audience to 'become involved in the process of responding' to the drama, which often, in these complex and harrowing plays, meant 'dealing with profoundly contradictory ideas and impulses' (Easterling 1997a: 164). Choruses often draw on mythology to set up analogies with the action of the play which encourage moral, religious and political reflection, or sing poetry whose imagery and symbolism enhances and deepens both the drama and the conflict of ideas in the play. Their songs create moods and evoke emotions central to the dramatic narrative. What they rarely do is offer mere narrative. The chorus has been taken to represent the voice of the democratic community, in tension with the individual (the conflict between the *demos* and the aristocrats was central to Athenian political life), but the choral odes were written in the Doric, not Athenian dialect, and often represented marginal groups such as slaves and women (Gagné and Hopman 2013: 23–4). The chorus were thus both in the drama as a fictional group of characters and outside the drama as ritual representatives of Athens in the Festival of Dionysus. They are the voice of the poet and the voice of the community (Gagné and Hopman 2013: 27), and they are also themselves.

All the performers wore masks, and exotic-looking, brightly coloured and decorated costumes. The masks were lightly constructed whole-head constructions, and their function was not to amplify the voice; they were part of the ritual costumes in the rite of Dionysus, in a manner not entirely dissimilar to the use of mask in some African or Haitian ritual. The costumes signified that the action was taking place in the heroic age of gods and heroes, not in the present, and often set away from Athenian soil. Indeed, the myths of the Trojan War and its aftermath figure large in the plays we know about. The setting of tragedies in the heroic past allowed the plays to reflect on Athenian concerns at a safe distance (perhaps in a similar way to how Shakespeare set his tragedies in Denmark or ancient Rome). We do, however, know of two plays which were set in contemporary times. Aeschylus' *Persians* (472 BCE) dramatised the Persians' defeat at the hands of their Greek enemies at the battle of Salamis. The dramatist Phrynicus wrote a lost play called *The Capture of Miletus* (494 BCE) about the destruction of the Greek city by the Persians. Notoriously, the author was fined and the play subsequently banned because the work 'reminded them of a disaster which touched them so closely'

(Herodotus 1972: 395). Some distance between the dramatic fiction and reality was apparently required to enable the reflection which was central to Greek tragedy.

Behind the acting area was the *skene*, a one-storey building with a central double door. Actors could enter from this door as if emerging from a building, or from the side aisles, when they would be entering from the open air: all the action in tragedy takes place outside. When the dramatist wanted to show what had happened inside the *skene* a wide trolley, the *ekkluklema*, could be rolled out from the central doors, typically to display the corpses of a killing that has just happened inside, such as when in Aeschylus' *Agamemnon* Clytemnestra gloats over the body of Agamemnon, the husband she has murdered alongside his concubine Cassandra (see below, p. 10; Aeschylus 2003: 92). A crane-like device, the *mechane*, could be used to fly actors as gods in the air, or to produce effects such as when the child-killer Medea escapes from Thebes in chariot pulled by dragons (see below, p. 27; Euripides 1997: 35).

In Athenian tragedy, then, a stylised depiction of human suffering was placed on display in the open air, but not simply for 'entertainment' or to evoke sentiment. Tragedy, many critics argue today, had an educational function for the good of the city: not to teach any kind of 'message', but to encourage emotionally engaged reflection on the nature of the values and ideals that were shared – or contested – within the community. In the darkest days of the long war with Sparta the comic dramatist Aristophanes wrote in his play *Frogs* about how Athens needed to bring back one of the great, but dead tragic poets from the underworld. Dionysus himself goes down to Hades. Euripides asks him why he needs a tragic poet. His answer shows how important tragedy was to the Athenians: 'to save the city, of course', is his reply (Aristophanes 1964: 208).

In this chapter we will look at one trilogy and five other plays which represent well what Greek tragedy meant to the people in the Theatre of Dionysus. We will also consider the responses of some important philosophers to Greek tragedy, responses which have been influential to thinking about tragedy in later years. Finally, we'll look at how the Romans developed tragedy in their own way.

Work from only three dramatists out of the hundreds who wrote for the Greek stage survives. Aeschylus (525–456 BCE) fought in the battle of Marathon against Persia. Since he increased the number of actors from one to two he can be seen as the founder of Greek tragedy. Sophocles (c. 496–406 BCE) was twice elected a general and was a priest of Aesculapius, the god of healing. Euripides (c. 485–406 BCE) was associated with radical thinkers and philosophical sceptics, men who cast doubt on the conventional religious and political views in the city. At the end of his life for some reason he left Athens for the court of the king of Macedonia.

AESCHYLUS, *THE ORESTEIA* (458 BCE)

Only one complete tragic trilogy of three plays written by a single author to be performed on one day of the Festival survives. The plays are *Agamemnon*, *The Libation Bearers* and *The Eumenides* by Aeschylus. Collectively they are known as *The Oresteia* since their central character is Orestes, the son of King Agamemnon of Argos.

Agamemnon had led the Greek forces in the war against Troy, a war fought to regain his brother's wife Helen, who had been abducted by Paris, prince of Troy. As the first play in the trilogy explains, before the Greek expedition could sail the goddess Artemis had demanded the sacrifice of Agamemnon's daughter Iphigenia in return for favourable winds. *Agamemnon* actually begins with a chain of beacons bringing news to the palace at Argos of the fall of Troy after ten years' fighting. Agamemnon's wife Clytemnestra has not, however, forgiven her husband for the killing of Iphigenia. She has taken as her lover Aegisthus, whose father, Thyestes, had been tricked into eating a meal of his own sons' flesh by Agamemnon's father Atreus, in vengeance for Thyestes seducing his wife. When Agamemnon arrives home with his slave and concubine, the Trojan prophetess Cassandra, Clytemnestra pretends to offer a welcome to her husband and persuades him to walk into the palace on a crimson tapestry. Once inside, she and Aegisthus murder Agamemnon and Cassandra and display their bodies to the city. The chorus of old men protest, but are powerless to act against both the murder and the seizure of power.

The second play, *The Libation Bearers*, begins with Electra, the daughter of Agamemnon and Clytemnestra, joining the chorus of the Queen's slaves pouring libations (ritual offerings of fluids, usually wine) on the tomb of Agamemnon. Her brother Orestes, who had not been in Argos when the murders took place, appears and identifies himself, and declares that the oracle of the god Apollo has ordered him to take vengeance for his father. With the collusion of Electra and the chorus, Aegisthus and Clytemnestra are killed by Orestes, and now their bodies are put on display. But at the very end Orestes is tormented by invisible Furies, the Erinyes, demon-like female avenging spirits demanding retribution for his mother's death.

The last part of the trilogy, *The Eumenides*, begins with Orestes, now in exile, seeking sanctuary at the shrine of Apollo at Delphi. But the chorus of Erinyes arrive in pursuit. Apollo seeks to protect him, and the goddess Athena arranges for a trial to settle the issue of whether vengeance must be taken on Orestes, to be judged by a panel of Athenian jurors. At the court of the Areopagus in Athens Orestes is acquitted on the strength of Athena's casting vote, and the Erinyes are pacified by Athena's offer that they become honoured guardians of the city, worshipped and offered tribute. They will in future be known as the Eumenides, 'the kindly ones'.

Written at a time when Athens was increasingly confident both in its own position at the head of the Greek world and also in its democratic institutions, the *Oresteia* has most frequently been read as offering a validation of the city's view of itself. In particular, the trilogy has been taken to show how the meaning of the Greek word *dike* ('justice'), is crucially refined through the progress of the dramatic action. Clytemnestra uses the term in its sense of 'vengeance' to justify the murder of her husband in retribution for the killing their daughter. Orestes also uses the term in this sense to account for his murder in turn of his mother Clytemnestra, only to bring the Erinyes onto his trail themselves demanding his destruction in the name of *dike* in the sense of 'right retribution' (vengeance can be excessive or cruel). But, when the citizen jurors of Athens – with the aid of the goddess Athena's casting vote – acquit Orestes and the pacified Erinyes agree to become guardian deities of the city, *dike* in the sense of legal justice is asserted as the resolution of the blood feud in the house of Atreus. The old aristocratic code of personal vengeance is tamed and civilised by the assertion of the voice of the community and the rule of law in history's first-ever murder trial. As the mid-twentieth-century critic H. D. F. Kitto (1966: 94) put it, 'the Areopagus, the prototype of all courts of justice, is a divine institution, a barrier against violence, anarchy, despotism: and at the first meeting of this court Athena sits with her fellow-citizens. Wrath ... gives place to Reason.' Athens shows its political system, also with divine approval, to be the culmination of a rational historical process. Edith Hall (2010: 211) writes that the play reflects:

> the real historical development of the archaic Greek city-state from the constitutional monarchy apparently portrayed in *Agamemnon*, through to the tyranny maintained by Clytemnestra and Aegisthus in *Libation-Bearers*, and thence to the Athenian democracy in *Eumenides*. This last play, uniquely in Greek tragedy, portrays a city that can govern herself without either tyrant or king.

Aeschylus' powerful pattern of dramatic symbolism across the trilogy can also be seen to work to reinforce this idea of a process which leads from violent, individualist turmoil to civic peace. The crimson tapestries on which Agamemnon walks as a **hubristic** monarch on his way to his murder in the first play (Aeschylus 2003: 77) are echoed in the civic crimson robes which the Erinyes wear as they process to their new home in a cave under the Acropolis (187). The chain of signal beacons which announce the destruction of Troy as an act of vengeance at the beginning of *Agamemnon* (54–5) has its structural counterpart in the torches carried by the religious procession of Athenian maidens who accompany the Erinyes as they exit as Eumenides at the end of the third play.

But not only Athenian democracy is promoted by this dramatic process. In deciding on the acquittal of Orestes, Athena's jury also validate Athenian patriarchy, the absolute dominance of men which was such a salient feature of Athenian society. In decreeing that Orestes should not be punished for killing his mother the play argues that 'fathers are more important than mothers, that men are more important than women, and that if women have a public role at all it is in religion rather than politics, legislation or law enforcement' (Hall 2010: 227).

This view of the *Oresteia* as a confident assertion of core Athenian values is opposed by the work of Simon Goldhill, who characteristically finds it more of a challenge to its audience. Goldhill analyses the different ways each character uses the notion of *dike* and finds no simple resolution or agreement that legal justice has superseded individualist vengeance by the end of the play. Indeed, the failure of characters to communicate with each other in the play is partly the result of a lack of a shared understanding of important words and concepts such as *dike*. Goldhill focuses on the role of Athena in casting her decisive vote. The fact is that the Athenian jurors cannot agree on whether Orestes should be punished. It takes decisive action from a female figure 'who transgresses the boundaries of sexual definition' (Goldhill 1986: 31), who deploys all the arts of **rhetorical** persuasion to win over the Erinyes, to close the action of the play. For Athena is a warrior goddess with no mother, a virgin who (in the most often repeated version of the myth) sprang fully armed from the forehead of her father Zeus, king of the gods. Because 'no mother gave me birth', she declares, 'in all things/ but marriage I wholeheartedly approve/ the male' (176–7). Just as the trilogy's narrative action is framed by effective dramatic symbols, so the figure of Athena at the trilogy's conclusion is structurally balanced by the figure of Clytemnestra in the trilogy's opening. She too displays the qualities associated with male warrior figures – bravery, a capacity for violence and a high sense of her own honour – and achieves her aims by a cunning use of rhetoric, in persuading Agamemnon to walk on the tapestries and enter the palace where he will be murdered. Rather than the play's ending asserting the dominance of the rational values of the community and the dominance of the male, writes Goldhill, 'the final reconciliation of divine and human forces in the city' (Goldhill 1986: 31) is achieved by a figure who doesn't fit the definitions to which a female or a citizen is supposed is conform in the 'rational' legal system of Athens. It's not law, but rhetoric, that brings resolution, and the power of language to make an argument not necessarily based on reason and evidence triumph in debate was a matter of considerable anxiety in a society where life and death political decisions were made in the debating chambers of the Assembly and law courts. Not a democratic majority, but a decision by a superior authority ends the blood feud. And 'the realignment of norms of sexual relations in the city is achieved through a figure who breaks across those norms' (Goldhill 1986: 31).

In this critical debate about the *Oresteia* can be seen a crucial question with regard to all tragedy: does it (or should it?) function to reinforce shared fundamental beliefs about society, community and human life, or does it challenge us to question the assumptions by which we live? In confronting the most difficult issues in life, tragedy acquires the authority to address these matters.

ARISTOTLE, *POETICS*

The surviving lecture notes of the Greek philosopher Aristotle (384–322 BCE) on the nature of poetry, known as the *Poetics*, have become one of the most influential contributions to the discussion of tragedy. As a scientist Aristotle was a great categoriser and in this text he sets out to explain what makes tragedy distinct from comedy and epic poetry (such as the *Iliad* and the *Odyssey* of Homer), and also to explain its different components and effects on its audience. He was also trying to defend poetry from the attacks of his teacher Plato, who saw poetry and drama as appealing to the lower, emotional parts of human nature, and as presenting mere imitations of a reality which he thought was just a second-hand experience of the eternal, unchanging truth, anyway. By 'poetry' he meant any kind of fictional narrative.

Aristotle was writing in the middle of the fourth century BCE, probably fifty or more years after the last play to be discussed in this chapter, and certainly well after the heyday of Athenian drama. His views are not to be taken as the authoritative statement on how the Greeks saw tragedy. In fact it is hard to use his views to explain and analyse such tragedies as Euripides' *Medea* (see below, p. 26) and *Bacchae* (see below, p. 31), for example. It was only after the publication of the translation and commentary by the Italian humanist Ludovico Castelvetro in 1570 that the *Poetics* came to be seen as a guide to Greek and to later tragedy. It was Castelvetro who laid down the rules that a tragedy should only represent the time it takes actually to play, that it should only have one location and only have a single plot (these strictures became known as the '**Unities**' of time, place and action). Aristotle never prescribes anything quite so precise (although it is the case that in almost all the plays that survive the action takes place in one day and in one location, Aeschylus' *Eumenides* (see above, p. 11) being a notable exception).

Aristotle says that all poetry, including tragedy, needs to tell us not what has happened, but the kind of things that *could* happen. In this way 'poetry utters universal truths' (Aristotle 2013: 28) about how people should behave in particular situations. Tragedy is about teaching us how to live. The 'moral element' of a tragedy and its 'ideas' are two of its six elements, along with the story, the poetic style, the staging and the music (24).

Aristotle defines a tragedy as 'a representation of an action of a superior kind – grand, and complete in itself – presented in embellished language, in distinct forms in different parts, performed by actors rather than told by a narrator, effecting, through pity and fear, the purification of such emotions'. (23) By 'superior' (the Greek *spoudaios*) he means that there should be a seriousness about the subject matter, but the word also suggests excellence and beauty. It's clear from the rest of the treatise that Aristotle also means that the main characters need also to be of superior social class, since notions of noble birth and virtue went closely together in Greek thought. A tragedy, he goes on to assert, must have a narrative which feels complete at the end and must be written in a language more ornate than the everyday. By 'different forms' and 'different parts' he is referring to the divisions in a Greek tragedy between the odes by the chorus which alternate with the 'episodes' of action performed by the actors. Each 'part' used different types of poetry distinguished by different metres (in Greek, this meant that there were particular patterns of long and short syllables in the lines).

Exactly what he means by the last part of his definition continues to cause controversy: the proposal that tragedy effects 'through pity and fear, the purification of such emotions'. It seems clear that Aristotle means that we feel pity for the characters who suffer in tragedy and fear in as much as we recognise that disaster can also happen to us. In particular, when suffering and death occur because of what people in family relationships do to one another he feels our emotions are more likely to be aroused (33). But what does 'purification' (*catharsis*) mean? A. D. Nuttall took the view that Aristotle was afraid of what emotion can make people do, and in tragedy 'it is not the emotions which are purified but the [human] organism' (Nuttall 1996: 6). Emotion is something which it is pleasurable to discharge since it is 'something we would wish to be rid of' (Nuttall 1996: 8). Anthony Kenny, on the other hand, does not regard Aristotle as such a thoroughgoing rationalist, but points out that elsewhere in his philosophy Aristotle thinks the virtuous man feels the right amount of emotion towards the appropriate object of that emotion (Kenny 2013: xxiv). Tragedy then purifies our emotions, since by painlessly feeling pity and fear in the theatre for fictional characters, and by comparing ourselves to them, we can 'calibrate the emotions of pity and fear when felt in real life. Watching tragedy helps us to put our own sorrows and worries into proportion, when we observe the catastrophes that have overtaken people far superior to the likes of ourselves' (Kenny 2013: xxvi). Aristotle makes it plain that 'tragedy is a representation of people who are better than we are' (36). Terry Eagleton takes a more cynical view, arguing that Aristotle saw tragedy as a means of producing tough-minded citizens who were ready to defend the state: 'Tragedy can perform the pleasurable, politically valuable service of draining off enfeebling emotions such as pity and fear, thus providing a kind of public therapy for those of the citizenry in danger of emotional flabbiness' (Eagleton 2003: 153).

There is less disagreement about Aristotle's other major pronouncements. He felt that a tragedy needed a main character, a 'protagonist', who was basically, but not 'especially good' yet possessing *megalopsychia*, 'greatness of soul'. He thought that if we saw a virtuous man falling from prosperity into catastrophe it would produce 'outrage' in the audience, who expect there to be some justice in the universe. On the other hand, if we see a bad man becoming prosperous and rewarded it is simply not tragic; nor is it tragic to see a wicked man falling from good fortune to bad, since this evokes neither pity nor fear. The tragic protagonist's fall happens because he or she 'errs in some way' (the Greek word used is **hamartia**, a mistake, not necessarily moral) (32). Incidentally, Aristotle does not write about a 'tragic flaw' in the protagonist's character leading to catastrophe; no such notion of 'character' in any case existed for the Greeks.

There should be a single action in the play to make the effect more powerful, leading to the point where the protagonist suffers a reversal of his or her hopes and expectations (the **peripeteia**). There will also often be the moment when the protagonist comes to understand a truth previously hidden from them which transforms their understanding of their situation. This moment of tragic recognition he called **anagnorisis**. Aristotle thought that it is most effective when the *peripeteia* and the *anagnorisis* happen at the same time, as in Sophocles' *Oedipus the King* (30) (see below, p. 18) when Oedipus's discovery that he has killed his own father and married his own mother precipitates his wife's suicide and his own self-blinding and fall from power (Sophocles 1982: 232ff.). But the outcome of the reversal of fortune and moment of recognition could also lead to a happy ending, as in Euripides' plays *Alcestis* and *Helen*, for example.

Aristotle's influence was perhaps strongest on late seventeenth-century tragic theatre (see below, p. 85), but his *Poetics* set out terms for talking about tragedy which are still useful.

SOPHOCLES, *OEDIPUS THE KING* (*c.* 425 BCE)

The story of Oedipus has become a powerful myth in the modern world because of its treatment by Sigmund Freud (see below, p. 118), but it also had great significance for the ancients. Sophocles' version takes place on the day when King Oedipus of Thebes finds out the truth of who he is. Thebes is afflicted by a terrible plague, and he sends his brother-in-law Creon to the oracle of the god Apollo to discover its source. Apollo's advice is apparently unambiguous: the murderer of the previous king, Laius, is still at large in the city, and until his polluted presence is driven out the plague will rage. Oedipus had become king shortly after Laius's death, having killed the Sphinx, the riddling monster which had been terrorising Thebes. He also married Laius's widow Jocasta. Oedipus sets out to find the killer, even if 'he proves to be an intimate of our house,/ here at my hearth' (Sophocles 1982: 172). When he came to Thebes Oedipus had been in self-imposed exile, having fled Corinth in fear of another statement from Apollo's oracle, that he would kill his father the king and marry his mother. But it emerges that an old man whom Oedipus has killed in a petty dispute at a crossroads on his way to Thebes was indeed Laius. It is then revealed that his Corinthian parents had secretly adopted him; that Jocasta is his true mother and Laius his father. Jocasta had commanded the baby Oedipus to be abandoned on Mount Cithaeron, his ankles pinned together, since an oracle of Apollo had foretold that the boy would grow up to be a father-killer. But Oedipus was found by a shepherd and handed to the childless King of Corinth, Polybus, to bring up as his own. When the truth is all too plain Jocasta hangs herself in despair. Oedipus takes the pins from her dress and blinds himself in their bedroom. Creon takes power in Thebes.

Of course Oedipus did not know who the old man at the crossroads was, nor had he any reason to think Jocasta might be his mother (Greek girls married older men at puberty, so there might only be fourteen or fifteen years between a husband and wife). The play seems to be suggesting that one cannot escape one's fate, and that terrible things can happen to undeserving people. There is no 'poetic justice', or the sense that the good will simply be rewarded and the bad punished in Greek tragedy. Oedipus is an energetic and popular leader, whose only desire seems to be to save his people from the plague. But he is short-tempered. Apart from the killing the old man (who had barged him off the road and struck Oedipus with his whip) (206), he insults and threatens the prophet Tiresias who has been goaded into trying to reveal the truth to the king (182), and he extracts the clinching information from a witness under threat of torture (229). He angrily suspects Creon of plotting against him (189). Some critics have suggested that these actions justify the terrible fate that Apollo has in store for him, but having a bad temper as a ruler and fearing conspiracies hardly seems to warrant such an appalling punishment (Hall 2010: 304). Older critics, somewhat bafflingly, have suggested that, even though Oedipus cannot be blamed for what he did unwittingly, he cannot rest unpunished for such deeds, and so we get a sense of divine justice at the end of the play even if we cannot quite comprehend it fully (Kitto 1966: 143).

In any case the Greeks would not have thought of Oedipus as the plaything of fate. Even if the idea might seem incoherent for a modern understanding of the term, the Greeks didn't think of fate (*moira*) as something that absolutely controlled all human actions. It may well have been the case that Oedipus was destined to kill his father and marry his mother, but he still chose to do what he did freely, they thought, and can still be held responsible for his actions. Divine foreknowledge doesn't compel human action. The blind Oedipus proudly proclaims as much to the chorus: 'Apollo, friends, Apollo – /he ordained my agonies … / But the hand that struck my eyes was mine.' (241). There is even a sense of heroic glory that Oedipus feels he was singled out by the gods for such a special demise.

The profoundly disturbing nature of the play prompted the French scholar Jean-Pierre Vernant (1983) to suggest that

Sophocles is prompting his audience to think hard about the boundaries of what it is to be a human and to live in a family and community. In the first part of the play, Oedipus's words often have a meaning he can't see which we can. When he says to his people that 'sick as you are, not one is as sick as I' (162), or that he will avenge Laius 'as if were my father' (173), we can see that Oedipus is a double character, a kind of riddle who means one thing to himself and another to the gods and to us. Even his name is a riddle. 'Oedipus' is the conventionally used Latin form of the name. The original Greek *Oidipous* means 'swollen foot' (referring to his infant injury), but it sounds as if it could also mean 'alas, to be two-footed', i.e. mortal, or, ironically, 'know where' (Goldhill 1986: 217). He is both hunter and hunted. He is both the city's saviour and its curse. He is two men in one, his own step-father and his own step-son. He is prayed to as a god by his people (160) but is also the beast (236) that must be driven from the city, like the sphinx which Oedipus himself slew. He is both the *turannos* (not quite our word 'tyrant', but a king who wins power himself) and the *pharmakos*, the scapegoat who must be ritually driven from the city to ensure its health. Mother-incest and father killing reverse the natural process of generation while erasing his own source of being, collapsing essential boundaries in human societies.

Vernant argues that in combining all these opposites in one person the boundaries between the human and the divine and between the human and the beast, between what gives health to the city and what must be expelled to maintain it become 'erased'. When Oedipus enquires into his own identity, he discovers that he is 'without fixed connection, without defined essence oscillating between the equal of god and the equal of nothing. His greatness consists in the very thing which expresses his enigmatic nature: the question.' (Vernant 1983: 208). Vernant's **postmodern** reading of the play finds in its structure an ability to bring into question fixed notions about what it is to be a human, a quality which has made it endure through time. In taking this critical approach he is also sharing in the spirit of Athenian tragedy, whose function was to confront the most difficult questions of existence by engaging the audience's emotions and thoughts with gripping and dramatically powerful performance.

SOPHOCLES, *ANTIGONE* (*c.* 442 BCE)

Although it tells the story of Oedipus's children, *Antigone* was written earlier than *Oedipus the King* and was not part of the same performance trilogy. In this play after Oedipus's death rule was shared between his two sons, Eteocles and Polynices. They quarrelled, and Polynices led an army from Argos to seize sole power in Thebes. Both sons are killed fighting each other. The Argive army is defeated and their uncle, Creon, becomes king. His first decree is to declare that the body of the traitor Polynices is not to have funeral rites, but to be left outside the city walls for the wild animals. In doing so he breaks a strong taboo in Greek culture – opposing armies always permitted the burial or cremation of each other's dead after battle – but also offends the shady and unnamed gods of the underworld, according to Oedipus's daughter Antigone. Athenian women had no political voice, but taking charge of funeral rites was one of the public religious duties they could exercise. Against the wishes of her sister Ismene, Antigone performs a ritual burial, is arrested and sentenced to death. The chorus, scared of Creon, hint at disapproval. Creon's own son, Haemon (who is engaged to Antigone), pleads for her pardon, citing the dissenting voice of the people, but Creon remains unbending. Only when the prophet Tiresias brings word that the gods disapprove – the animal sacrifice he is carrying out goes ominously wrong – does Creon, at the chorus's prompting, change his mind. But it is too late. Antigone, sentenced to be walled up alive in a rock, has hanged herself with her bridal veil. Haemon spits in his father's face and stabs himself. Creon's wife Eurydice also takes her own life, leaving the king broken and distraught.

Since the nineteenth-century German philosopher Hegel's work on the play (see below, p. 24), this tragedy has very often been seen as a clash of incompatible principles, with critics taking one side or the other (but mostly Antigone's). She has been taken to stand for the sacredness of family ties, for the nurturing female, for the individual conscience against the all-powerful state, for the religious conscience, for youth and for heroic self-sacrifice. Creon has been taken to represent the power of the state (for good or ill), male authority, political authoritarianism and the arrogance of power and age. The fact that Antigone seems to have the gods on her side (though they do not save her life) might suggest that the play prompts us to take her side in the conflict.

But this reading imposes more modern liberal notions on a complex ancient drama and irons out the challenge to the audience which is the hallmark of Greek tragedy. The idea that the play is a simple conflict between the claims of the family and the claims of the city has rightly been called 'a bold misreading of the play' (Carter 2007: 111). Creon requires obedience to his command because the safety of the individual and the family in fact depended upon the security of the whole city (68). It is important to recognise that all Greek cities were in genuine danger of conquest and destruction from their rival cities. When he compares the city to a warship (steered by him) whose oarsmen must row together (67), or to the line of spearmen in battle whose survival depends upon no one breaking ranks (94), he is using language that his citizen-warrior audience would affirm from personal experience. We know from the historian Thucydides that the pre-eminent Athenian statesman of the time, Pericles, declared that putting one's family before the city could endanger everyone (Carter 2007: 108). The idea that one's conscience can override the law, no matter how that law was created, was not a Greek one, either – the philosopher Socrates went to his death emphasising that point (Plato 1969: 83ff). It may be the case that the audience would have doubts about Creon's legitimacy as a ruler, but the dominant idea was that rulers should be obeyed.

The challenging conflict in the play can rather be seen to be between historical conceptions of loyalty. Greek morality was focused on duties created by bonds of personal duty to others. For Creon, the prior moral claim on the inhabitants of Thebes is clearly that of the city. This was a widely held view in contemporary democratic Athens. As Pericles put it, 'we do not say that a man who takes no interest in politics is a man who minds his own business; we say that he has no business here at all.' (Thucydides 1972: 147) 'Politics' here is used to render '*ta politika*', the affairs of the city. Athens was a democracy from which women were barred. Creon also finds Antigone's challenge to his political authority a challenge to the rule of men (86). But Antigone's primary loyalty is to her blood relations, even before a husband and children (Sophocles 1982: 105). For her, the primary moral bond is not the one most valued by the contemporary, fifth-century BCE state, but rather that of the heroic age as written about by the poet Homer in the *Iliad* and the *Odyssey* (Goldhill 1986: 91).

For the Greeks Homer was seen as the repository of their values. His heroes showed how a man ought to live, and there were moral and political lessons to be learnt from his stories. Greek tragedies were almost all set in the heroic age which he depicts. The whole of these poems was regularly recited at city festivals. Politicians and poets cited Homer to support and illustrate their ideas. But fifth-century BCE Athens was very different from bronze-age Greece. Its leaders did not rule as warrior aristocrats, but as elected generals. Its men did not fight in single combat, but as a unit, shoulder-to-shoulder in the line of battle. Sophocles' *Antigone* exposes a contradiction between the dominant, universally acknowledged values of the foundation texts of the culture and the real political conditions in which people lived. It asks its audience to consider that contradiction. The gods seem to favour Antigone's side, but considerable sympathy is created for Creon in the play's conclusion. He even drops his anxious autocratic stance and listens wisely to his advisers in a way more congenial to the Athenian democrats (117). Yet the woman clearly does also triumph in a most disturbing way for its original audience. Her reported death scene is a kind of inverted wedding scene; her cave is her 'bridal-bed' (105) where it is the man who is penetrated and bleeds (122).

The tragic conflict which destroys both Antigone and Creon can be seen as the product of contradictions in the stories a society tells about itself, which is another way of saying its **ideology**. Tragedy can often arise when political and social change moves faster than the dominant stories, and ideological fissures arise. The Irish playwright Brian Friel in his tragedy *Translations* talks of how 'it can happen that a civilization can become imprisoned in a linguistic contour which no longer matches the landscape of ... fact' (Friel 1996: 419). Antigone is imprisoned in such a 'contour', and it has tragic consequences for all around her. Sophocles' play dramatises the clash between the heroic map of Greek life and its real Athenian social landscape.

HEGEL ON TRAGEDY

The German philosopher G. W. F. Hegel (1770–1831) said that Sophocles' *Antigone* was 'one of the most sublime and in every respect most excellent works of art of all time' (cited in Stern 2013: 160). He wrote about the tragedy several times in his works but in his *Phenomenology of Spirit* (1807) he uses the play to explain a particular point about the development of the ancient Greek view of people's place in the world and of their relations with each other. But Hegel's reading of *Antigone* has had an important influence on the way people think about tragedy in general.

Throughout Hegel's work he explains how philosophy can make us see that the universe is not a chaotic and hostile place but an inherently rational order in which we can eventually feel at home and be free. In order to do this we first have to discover that the problems we have in perceiving that the world is rational and comprehensible are the result of thinking about it in the wrong way, through a framework of one-sided, contradictory opposites: 'we believe that something is *either* finite *or* infinite, one *or* many, free *or* necessitated, human *or* divine, autonomous *or* part of a community, and so on' (Stern 2013: 14). We have to make these mistakes in order to move forward to the 'dialectical' way of thought which Hegel propounds, in which we see that that these terms are not in fact mutually exclusive, and then, rather than despairing of understanding the world and doubting human knowledge, we can see that the world is rational and knowable to us as rational beings. It's important here that Hegel sees the development of human understanding, of human mind and consciousness (he uses the German word *geist*, 'spirit', here) as a historical process happening in time. It's also significant, as Terry Eagleton observes, that the development of consciousness through error is itself a tragic process (Eagleton 2003: 42). Finally, Hegel does believe that the development of human consciousness through time is a rational process which will lead to a humanity which is free, at home with itself and with a full understanding of the world.

In *The Phenomenology of Spirit* Hegel writes how in ancient Greece men and women originally did not see themselves as individuals but as unselfconscious embodiments of the sphere in society in which they lived. Antigone as a woman lives according to the 'divine law', which governs families and human relations with the gods. Creon, as a male ruler, lives according to the 'human law', which regulates the political life of the wider community. There had been a harmony between these two spheres, with each complementing the other. But conflict arises in the figure of the dead Polynices, who is both a male with political significance but also a brother and part of the female sphere. The 'ethical order' – the moral conception of each sphere – comes into conflict, and no resolution is possible because both Antigone and Creon only understand their place in the world through the sphere in which they live and in which their consciousness is realised. The conflict is not between individual and state, or between virtue and tyranny, but between two one-sided positions, each of which embodies some good. In fact the 'particular individual' in this scheme 'counts only as a shadowy unreality' (cited in Stern 2013: 163) in the greater development of human consciousness which is unfolding in this tragedy.

Tragedy is the result of larger historical forces which the individual cannot see beyond in his or her predicament, part of the one-sided way of understanding the world which human beings have to work through on their progress towards freedom and complete understanding. Hegel writes that the next stage of human development which emerges from this tragic conflict in the ancient world is the 'shattering' of the community into which the individual had been fully absorbed and the emergence of the self-conscious person in his or her own right (Stern 2013: 167).

The idea that tragedy is not the result of fate or individual choice, but of the operation of larger, historical forces which are in conflict and which lead to individual suffering has been developed by later critics, especially in the Marxist tradition (see, for example, below p. 77). Hegel believed that it was only in certain periods of historical transition when new forms of consciousness arose that genuine tragedy can be written, in particular, when classical Greek culture lost its complete sense of organic unity and also when the medieval world gave way to the modern in the time of Shakespeare. At the moment when a culture devotes its 'spiritual energies' almost exclusively to art, he believed, people then realise they need more than the arts to satisfy them (Paolucci 1962: xv). These are the moments, he thought, when tragedy, the most self-critical art arose.

Because Hegel sees tragedy as part of a process leading to the triumph of reason, the 'necessary' suffering of the individual is rather downplayed, since the sufferer is in pain but cannot see how history is working through their suffering towards its goal: 'The necessity of all that particular individuals experience is able (in tragedy) to appear in complete concord with reason' (cited in Eagleton 2003: 43). So there is a sense in which Hegel's theory explains tragedy only finally to discount what for most people is its tragic nature: grief, pain, anguish, misery. There is perhaps something callous, even sinister about this, as Adrian Poole points out (Poole 2005: 59).

It is also evident that Hegel's theory of tragedy as the clash of irreconcilable historical forces on the way to the victory of the rational does not apply to all tragedies, let alone Greek ones. The triumph of the god Dionysus in Euripides' *Bacchae* (see below, p. 31) is a prime example.

EURIPIDES, *MEDEA* (431 BCE)

When this shocking play was first performed the jurors placed the trilogy of which it was part third and last. Euripides had taken the myth of the foreign wife of the hero Jason and turned it into something very disturbing.

Jason had led a group of heroes known as the Argonauts to Colchis, on the northern shore of the Black Sea, to steal the Golden Fleece. There he was aided by the King's daughter, Medea. She killed her own brother in order to help her lover Jason escape and then, back in Greece, arranged the murder of Pelias, the king who had usurped the throne of Jason's father. When the play begins Jason and Medea are in Corinth. They are married, with two children, but Jason has announced that he is leaving Medea to marry Glauce, the young daughter of Creon, King of Corinth (this is a common name for kings in tragedy – the word *kreiōn* in Greek meant a ruler). It was far from uncommon, and in fact uncontroversial, for Athenian men to divorce their wives for more valuable partners, but Medea is devastated by the news. Creon, who is wary of her, wants her out of his territory, but he is persuaded by Medea to let her stay one more day. Having vented her feelings at her betrayal to Jason and secured the guarantee of Aegeus, King of Athens, for a place of refuge, she falsely tells Jason that she now accepts the situation and sends some gifts to his new wife: a crown and robe. These turn out to be coated with a deadly poison which burns and eats away the flesh of Glauce and even destroys Creon when he embraces his dying daughter. Medea then enacts what she feels will hurt Jason the most: she kills their two sons. A broken Jason confronts her at the end of the play, as she leaves for Athens with their children's bodies in a flying chariot pulled by dragons provided by her grandfather, Helios the sun-god.

In other versions of the myth, it was the Corinthians, not Medea, who killed the children in vengeance for Medea killing Creon, or she killed them by accident in trying to make them immortal by some magic process (Knox 1983: 272–3). It is Euripides who makes Medea the deliberate child-killer who not only gets away with her crime, but is aided in her flight by the gods themselves. Members of the contemporary audience could certainly have read the play as endorsing some dominant misogynistic ideas. The play could be seen as a warning about what happens when a woman is left outside male control (*kureia*, lordship as it was known) (Hall 2010: 192), or even a dire statement of the disorder that can happen in a woman's mind when her health is damaged by a lack of sex (Hall 2010: 134).

This contemporary medical belief is what the crass Jason thinks is her problem (Euripides 1997: 36).

But Euripides does not present Medea as a deranged, emotionally unhinged woman or as one motivated by a manic sexual jealousy. She is given a long, dramatically powerful speech where she debates with herself in torment whether she can bear to kill her children (28–9). Euripides puts on stage in the person of Medea an 'unprecedented degree' of internalised self-consciousness, a real sense of psychological interiority which not only represented a great advance in dramatic art but must also have encouraged some understanding if not quite sympathy from the male audience (Hall 2010: 192). Furthermore, it is quite clear that Medea does not call on the gods to assist her in her vengeance because Jason has broken her heart, but because he has broken his oaths to her as husband (Kerrigan 1996: 91). It is her honour, her pride, her sense that others will no longer be jealous of her – in fact that people will now laugh at her (36) – that drives her to ensure that he is hurt just as much as she is. 'Why did you kill them?' asks Jason, ultimately. 'To cause you pain' is her blunt reply (38). Like Antigone (see above, p. 21) Medea's values are those not of a woman, but of a Homeric hero like Sophocles' Ajax in the play of that name, whose pride has been injured and who must have vengeance. In epic poetry, just as Odysseus had a right to take bloody vengeance when his honour was damaged by the suitors pursuing Odysseus's wife Penelope in the *Odyssey*, so Medea demands her right to retribution (Knox 1983: 277). Dishonour in marriage is, in Medea's words, not 'a small hurt for a woman' (37). That she sees herself as living by the code of a male hero is more than evident in her words to the chorus: 'let no-one think of me as weak and submissive, a cipher – but as a woman of a very different kind, dangerous to my enemies and good to my friends. Such people's lives win the greatest renown' (22). Some audience members may have felt that in adopting heroic male values she becomes a monster, but others may be prompted to think about why what is so admirable in a man is so wicked in a woman. Homeric values are once again challenged by being attributed to a woman; or perhaps the status of a woman is enhanced by attributing Homeric values to her.

It is clear, moreover, that Medea is more than a woman. She calls on the gods to help her enact her vengeance, and she succeeds. Her final appearance in the sun-god's chariot, probably suspended above the stage on the *mechane* (see above, p. 9) puts her exactly where Euripides places the gods who come to resolve the action in many of his plays, such as when Dionysus finally appears as himself in the *Bacchae* (see below, p. 31). There is something divine about Medea.

Euripides was apparently regarded as a misogynist because of his portrayal of women like Medea, most notably by the comic dramatist Aristophanes (Aristophanes 1964: 117). But it is certainly possible to read the play in completely the opposite fashion. Writing in 1977, at a high-point in feminist political activism, Bernard Knox wrote that 'the play is very much concerned with the problem of women's place in human society … The *Medea* is not about woman's rights; it is about woman's wrongs, those done to her and by her' (Knox 1983: 283). Medea's great speech about how unequal is the institution of marriage, and the shallowness and danger of women's lives, is a most powerful statement of the injustice of female inequality in Athens (7–8). The Chorus of Corinthian women cannot condone the killings, but their sympathy for her position is constant. They look forward to the day when women will be able to tell their own story, 'free from the bitter tongue of [men's] slander' (12). Knox (1983: 293) writes that when all that is Medea's life as a woman is betrayed by Jason, all her energy and power turns:

> into a deadly instrument to destroy him. It became a *theos* [god, a divine presence], relentless, merciless force, the unspeakable violence of the oppressed and betrayed, which, because it has been so long pent up, carries everything before it to destruction, even if it also destroys what it loves most.

Knox is taking the view that tragedy here is a direct expression of historical and political forces; that it can show how the human energies that resist injustice and inequality will become distorted in oppressive societies and will emerge as tragic suffering in literature. In this he can be seen to have ideas in common with the materialist critics of the late twentieth century (see below, p. 77). The roots of tragedy lie not in abstract ideas about the general human condition, or in fate, or in the working out of divine will, as Hegel thought, but in the injustices of the society that produces a tragedy. What is significant is that tragedy can then be seen to be looking forward to how injustice might be ended. As Aristotle taught, it can teach us how better to live.

WOMEN IN TRAGEDY

In Athens respectable married women did not leave their home unaccompanied, and may even have gone veiled in public. Their sphere was indoors, under the guardianship of their master, their *kurios*. Tragedy seems to occur when the doors of the *skene* at the back of stage open and women come out into the public space. *Antigone* begins with two unaccompanied, unmarried women going outside the walls of the city itself where one at least plans subversion of male power (Sophocles 1982: 60). Athenian women could not attend the assembly, or the law courts; it seems likely that very few, if any, attended the theatre. Yet women play central and crucial roles in the public and political events which constitute the narratives of Athenian drama.

To explain this strange situation it has been suggested that female avengers such as Clytemnestra or Medea, or those women taking an active role in political events – such as Antigone or Jocasta – represent a repressed sense of the unacknowledged potential and voice of women. At any rate they point to 'a general sense of anxiety about women, stemming from the anomalous position they occupied in Athenian society' (Blundell 1995: 180). The critic Froma Zeitlin explains this matter in a different way. Since tragedy sets out to explore crucial questions in Athenian life, the prominent position of women on stage serves to provide a set of opposing qualities against which men's sense of their identity as men can be explored: 'the woman is assigned the role of the radical other' (Zeitlin 1996: 346). The plays are not interested in women in their own right, but as a means of exploring masculine identity through contrast. When men are passive or grieving, when they show pity or fear on stage, they are entering characteristically female territory, and posing the unsettling question to the audience of where the boundary between socially approved masculine and feminine behaviour should be set. Zeitlin suggests that tragedy might paradoxically be using 'the feminine for the purposes of imagining a fuller model of the masculine self' (Zeitlin 1996: 363).

In any case, the prominence of women on stage may have been because the Greeks saw the theatre as, in a sense, feminine. According to myth, women were created in imitation of men, 'adorned with deceptive allure' (Zeitlin 1996: 362). The theatre was imitation, and tragedy's female characters are typically conniving and false. The women's realm is not the outdoor, public life of men, but the household, a private interior space that 'equips them for deviousness and duplicity' (Zeitlin 1996: 357). The interior of the *skene* at the back of the stage from which women emerge stands for the hidden fate which is unknown to the protagonist at the beginning of the action. Female characters are often the chief plotters within the play, or the controllers of the play within the play. The conflicts, and even the form of tragedies represent the deep structures of the society which created them, often in subtle but powerful ways.

EURIPIDES, *BACCHAE* (405 BCE)

The *Bacchae* was first performed after Euripides' death, just before Athens' final defeat in the long war with Sparta. 'Bacchae', or Bacchants, are female devotees of the god Dionysus, son of Zeus (see above, p. 5). The play begins as the god himself, in disguise as a stranger, arrives at Thebes with his chorus of followers from Lydia, a 'barbarian' country in Asia Minor. The women of Thebes, including Agaüe, the mother of King Pentheus, have also become Bacchae and have left the city for the woods of Mount Cithaeron, dressed in fawn skins and waving the ritual thyrsus, a staff made of a fennel stalk and topped with ivy. Bacchic worship involves ecstatic singing and dancing and communing with nature, but it can also climax in the ritual tearing apart of animals (*sparagmos*).

King Pentheus is hostile to the stranger and determined to bring the women back under control. Even his grandfather Cadmus and the blind seer Tiresias want to join the revels, dressed in Bacchic clothes. Pentheus is in fact Dionysus's cousin; his mother Agauë is sister to the god's mortal mother Semele. Pentheus arrests the stranger and puts him under guard, but he escapes from prison, and an earthquake destroys the King's palace. News comes that after a bout of *sparagmos* the women of Thebes have plundered two nearby towns, invulnerable to male weapons. Pentheus is about to send his forces to take action, when the stranger suddenly brings the King under his spell, and persuades him to disguise himself as a woman to spy upon the Bacchae. Pentheus does so, and the messenger reports how the King was then discovered and torn to pieces by the Bacchae. Agauë his mother enters, with her own son's head in her hands, saying it is that of a lion. Dionysus takes her out of her trance, and then appears in the air above the stage as himself, proclaiming that he has punished Thebes for not accepting his worship. The rest of Pentheus's dismembered body is brought on stage to be reassembled. The god is remorseless and triumphant. Exile and transformation await the agonised Agauë and Cadmus.

The *Bacchae* is perhaps the strangest and the most troubling of the ancient Greek tragedies that survive. Modern criticism of the play has been strongly influenced by the German philosopher Friedrich Nietzsche's account of Dionysus in his 1872 book *The Birth of Tragedy* (see below, p. 34). For Nietzsche, Dionysus stood for not just the sense of leaving one's identity behind through intoxication or dance or theatrical experience, but for the joyful but terrifying loss of individual identity itself. In late-twentieth-century criticism Dionysus comes to stand for the 'Other', the opposite of all the dominant identities in society which structure that society and the way power is shared out. As the French classicist Jean-Paul Vernant would put it, 'to the male, Dionysus will be female, to the Greek he will be barbarian, to humans, divine and thus always Other, forever changing into whatever one least knows' (Mills 2006: 90; Vernant 1988: 398–400). This erasing of distinctions is expressed in the play by the prophet

Tiresias himself when he says that Dionysus 'wishes to be honoured and exalted/ By all alike, and no one is excluded.' (Euripides 2009: 252). In all the plays in which he appears Tiresias always speaks the truth. Pentheus is a rigid, authoritarian monarch in the model of Creon in Sophocles' *Antigone* (see above, p. 21) whose destruction at the hands of Dionysus (having been made to dress as a woman) could be read as a victory for a democratic god in whose name the patriarchal Athenians are gathered, a god who nevertheless hates all distinctions of status (Mills 2006: 97). But if Dionysus stands for a much more radical principle than that, as Nietzsche suggested, then this tragedy seeks to challenge its audience into confronting a force which might either be seen as something deep within the human mind or as the inexplicable of nature of what it is to be a god – or both at the same time, for Greek gods were both individual beings and qualities that existed in the world and in people.

Civilisation, restraint, social hierarchy: if these things are abandoned, it seems, great joy and freedom can be achieved in a life of dance and ecstasy. The earth itself yields up wine and honey to the Maenads on Mount Cithaeron and they suckle wild animals in harmony with nature, their faces licked by snakes (270). But at the command of the god these same women rip Pentheus to pieces and their leader Agauë is made to tear the head off her own son. She and her father Cadmus accept the god's rule but are still punished without mercy merely because Cadmus had said that Dionysus had a mortal father, not Zeus (297). Dionysus is a liberator but he is also cruel and deceitful and takes delight in that deceit. The play features wild dancing and fine poetry sung by the chorus; it puts on stage comic old men in the form of Cadmus and Tiresias in drag, but it also contains horror and brutality. To the Greeks the tragic truth expressed by the play may have been the contradictory, inexplicable nature of divinity. In this way tragedy might be seen as a way of offering an explanation of suffering in the world, rather than admitting it to be random and meaningless.

To modern readers and critics Pentheus's surrender to Dionysus can look more like an acceptance of repressed psychological needs (Goldhill 1997b: 342). Is his hatred of all the god stands for so aggressive because he is repressing his real desires, either a need to shake off duty and authority and revel in the woods, or possibly even homosexual feelings? Dionysus is sexually ambivalent in appearance, protests Pentheus often (253, 261), and when Pentheus wrestles the 'bull' (representing male sexuality) there could certainly be some subtextual meaning (267). There might even be repressed incestuous desire towards his mother, for he seems keen to overlook what he takes to be the sexual activities of the Bacchants of whom she is the leader (281). This **psychoanalytical** view locates the tragedy in the structure of the human mind itself, a tragic view of the human consciousness divided against itself through the very process of socialisation, the way in which the individual becomes a part of human society (see below, p. 159). Pentheus has been brought up in a society where he cannot, or even should not acknowledge his own unacknowledged needs and feelings.

The *Bacchae* is the earliest play in the Western tradition which locates tragedy in something dark and violent, yet perversely desirable in human life which reason and culture cannot drive out.

NIETZSCHE, *THE BIRTH OF TRAGEDY* (1872)

The German philosopher Friedrich Nietzsche's first major work was a study of the forces which he claimed made the tragedies of Aeschylus and Sophocles such supreme achievements. Nietzsche was not alone at the time in thinking that the culture of fifth-century BCE Athens was a high-point in human history (Nietzsche 1999: 72), with tragedy standing at its artistic zenith. But he also felt that German culture had the potential to rival that of the Greeks, and in particular he felt that the music-theatre of his friend Richard Wagner (to whom he dedicated *The Birth of Tragedy*) could restore tragedy to what it had been for the Athenians.

At this time Nietzsche's ideas about the nature of human experience were under the influence of Arthur Schopenhauer. Schopenhauer taught that what we think we perceive in time and space is an illusion generated by the workings of an entity called 'the Will', which is the true underlying reality of the world. The Will holds each human in its control and drives our desires and actions in such a way as to make happiness impossible. Only when contemplating art can we escape the frustrations and miseries of life, since art is 'radically disinterested' in the struggles of the Will (Geuss 1999: vii). Music, since it doesn't represent the world as other art forms do, was claimed by Schopenhauer to give us direct access to the ultimate reality beyond the illusory world of the senses, and thus to be in tune with the Will itself and so able to escape its demands upon us.

Nietzsche wrote that what made Greek tragedy so powerful artistically was its combination of music and words. He rejected the idea that we should consider the moral or intellectual content of tragedy; it is an aesthetic experience. He identified the flute-accompanied singing of the chorus with the presence of the god Dionysus, and the spoken words and performance of the actors with the god Apollo. Dionysus stood for the ecstatic loss of individuality, a wild, irrational abandonment of self in music and dancing. This loss of self is terrifying but also pleasurable, since it offers direct access to the ultimate reality of the Will. When we are lost in the Dionysiac music of the chorus:

> for brief moments we are truly the primordial being itself and we feel its unbounded greed and lust for being; the struggle, the agony, the destruction of appearances ... [but we also] become one with the immeasurable, primordial delight in existence, and receive an intimation, in Dionysiac ecstasy, that this delight is indestructible and eternal. Despite pity and fear, we are happily alive, not as individuals, but as the *one* living being ...
>
> (81)

In fact we would be unable to bear the unadulterated experience of Dionysiac music, so we need the presence of Apollo, who stood for the contrary principle: the individual self and also the individual, representational work of art, a notion which also includes the actor's performance. But the Apollonian idea that we are truly individuals separate from the world around us he thought an illusion. In Greek tragedy Dionysus and Apollo came together in harmony, to give the appearance of true insight into the world:

> with the enormous force of image, concept, ethical concept and sympathetic excitement, the Apolline wrenches man out his orgiastic self-destruction, deceives him about the generality of the Dionysiac event, and induces him into a delusion that he is seeing a single image of the world ... and is simply meant to *see* it better and with greater inward involvement *thanks to the music.*
>
> (102)

Tragedy enables its audience to see momentarily that suffering and death are part of the nature of the universe, but to see that suffering from the point of view of the unindividuated, self-delighting and playful universe itself, as well as from the point of view of the heroic individual protagonist. Nietzsche cites a comparison made by the Greek philosopher Heraclitus, who said 'the force that shapes the world' is like 'a playing child who ... builds up piles of sand only to knock them down again' (114). Tragedy allows us to have the valuable impression that there is joy (as well as terror) in destruction, even our own, rather than face the simple truth as baldly stated by the satyr Silenus, when, according to Aristotle, he was forced by King Midas to tell what is 'the best and most excellent thing for human beings'. With a shrill laugh he answers that 'the very best thing is ... not to have been born, not to *be*, to be *nothing*. However, the second best thing for you is: to die soon.' (23) Tragedy allows us to delight in this horrible 'truth'; it offers us a 'metaphysical supplement to the reality of nature' so that we can 'overcome' it. (113) In this way Nietzsche justifies his claim that genuine tragedy is the highest art form, and explains how can take delight in watching the suffering of others, and even in contemplating our own death.

Genuine tragedy ended in Greece when the philosopher Socrates sought to explain the world rationally and, according to Nietzsche, laid the foundations of the modern (but mistaken) scientific world view that the world can be understood and made a place where we can be at home and content. Nietzsche believed that Euripides was infected by the ideas of his friend Socrates and wrote plays about mere individuals, not about the mythic figures of Aeschylus and Sophocles who stood for more profound eternal truths about human existence. Euripides' *Bacchae* (see above, p. 31) represented a final admission, Nietzsche wrote, that Dionsyus had a power he had foolishly neglected in his rationalist tragedies (60). Though Nietzsche later seemed to change his mind, the new mythology-based operas of Richard Wagner, where every word was sung to what Nietzsche believed to be sublime music, would restore to the German people, he claimed, the experience of genuine tragedy.

Although few today would regard Nietzsche's account of the origins of tragedy as historically accurate, nor regard music as having such huge power to grant metaphysical understanding, his identification of irrational, destructive forces existing deep in the human mind, and of a potential delight in such forces, has been important in thinking about tragedy since his book became more widely known in the early twentieth century. In 1872, *The Death of Tragedy* suffered universally hostile reviews.

Tragedy continued to be written in Greece in the centuries after Sophocles' death, but none of it has survived in more than fragments. The plays we have owe their preservation to recognition of their excellence in some way. They were copied out to be used in schools.

CONTEXTS: SENECA AND ROMAN TRAGEDY

Rome's relationship with Greek culture was complex. As the empire expanded in the third and second centuries BCE, Roman armies conquered all but the most distant Greek territories. The various Greek communities scattered over the Mediterranean basin and beyond lacked the political and military strength to resist the Romans, but their culture possessed a prestige and pre-eminence that the Romans could not emulate. Instead they appropriated it. Wealthy and powerful Romans wanted to be associated with Greek forms of architecture, art, drama, literature or philosophy in order to enhance their status, to show that they were more than just military leaders or effective political operators. From the third century BCE Latin tragedies based on fourth-century Greek models were performed for the public at festivals paid for by wealthy or powerful Romans. Though there was some opposition from traditionalists who saw the theatre as effete and unmanly, eventually a permanent stone theatre, the Theatre of Pompey, opened in Rome in 55 BCE.

Roman theatres in Seneca's day had deep semi-circular stages, with the audience rising in tiers above the performance area. A great linen awning protected the spectators from the elements. There was a drop-curtain which was raised at the beginning and lowered at the end of the performance. Sets were elaborate and highly decorated. There was still a chorus, but it had shrunk in size to no more than half a dozen, and it did not necessarily stay on stage throughout the performance as it had in the Athenian theatre.

The only complete Roman tragedies that survive are by Lucius Annaeus Seneca (c. 4 BCE–65 CE). Seneca was born into the Roman elite and was active at court during the turbulent and dangerous regimes of the emperors Caligula, Claudius and Nero. After eight years of exile he became the speechwriter and adviser for Nero. Seneca was ultimately forced to commit suicide when he was accused of being part of a conspiracy against the emperor. He lost influence, it seems, when he was lukewarm about helping Nero kill his own mother (Seneca 2010: x). Seneca's tragedies reflect his experiences: they are set in a world of violent, vengeful and cruel monarchs and their families, where passions are uncontrollable. Roman political life was highly theatrical. Noblemen were highly trained in the art of rhetoric, and processions, displays and public ceremonies were a crucial means by which political authority was asserted. Seneca's characters also declaim their speeches in what sounds like highly crafted public oratory. The violence and spectacle of gladiatorial combat and the Roman triumph have their counterpart in the violence and spectacle so eloquently described in the rhetoric of Seneca's characters.

Yet Seneca's other writings are notable for propounding the Stoic philosophy. Originating in Greece in the late third century BCE, the Stoics taught that the world was rationally ordered by a benevolent divine force, and that we could not alter how events unfold in that world. Happiness could be found by living in accordance with nature, by accepting that what happens is part of that rational, natural order, and by valuing only virtue itself as ultimately worth having. Excess emotion in response to the events of one's life was pointless. Yet Seneca's tragedies show a very different world, where there is little sign that the world is unfolding in a rational way, where passion and cruelty predominate, and where the innocent and the guilty suffer alike.

It has often been argued that Seneca's tragedies were not written for full theatrical performance, but for recitation in private houses. However, there are many good reasons, not least in the highly theatrical qualities of the plays themselves, to believe that they were fully staged in Roman theatres (Boyle 1997: 11).

SENECA, *PHAEDRA* (45 CE?)

Phaedra's major source is Euripides' tragedy *Hippolytus*. Phaedra, wife of Theseus, King of Athens, has conceived a passionate desire for her own stepson Hippolytus, a misogynist who prefers hunting in the wild to any other activity. Her husband has gone down into the underworld to help his friend Pirithous steal the wife of Hades, king of that region. The desperate Phaedra considers suicide, but her old nurse hopefully tries to persuade Hippolytus to show some interest in 'the pleasures of Venus', the goddess of sexual love (Seneca 2010: 15). He rejects her views, and, when Phaedra herself declares her love, he grabs her by the hair and is about to stab her when he leaves the stage in disgust at her acquiescence in death, leaving his 'tainted sword' behind (22). The Nurse persuades Phaedra to claim she has been raped by Hippolytus. At this point Theseus returns and Phaedra shows him the sword as proof she has been assaulted. Theseus calls on his father the sea-god Neptune to grant him a promised wish and destroy his stepson. The messenger then tells how a monstrous bull arose from the sea and terrified the horses of Hippolytus's chariot. They bolted, overturning the vehicle. Trapped in the reins, Hippolytus was dragged to a violent death. On hearing the news, Phaedra admits Hippolytus's innocence and commits suicide. Theseus is left to assemble the shattered remains of his stepson's body.

If tragedy in democratic Athens sought to make the citizens reflect upon questions and issues central to their public lives, there is no such debate in Seneca. In *Phaedra* there is a focus on the inner obsessions and emotions of the characters, and in the cruel and authoritarian monarchy of Imperial Rome there is a single powerful view of human life being propounded. Seneca draws on a convention of late Greek and Roman comedy, the use of **soliloquy** and aside, to give the audience insight into the thoughts and feelings of his protagonists. Phaedra's opening speech (5–6) seems as likely to be addressed to the audience as to the Nurse (no stage directions appear in the ancient manuscripts on which modern texts are ultimately based). Her intricate and striking rhetoric powerfully conveys the tortured nature of her mind, overwhelmed by a passion she knows is wrong. In addition, as A. J. Boyle puts it, 'she does not so much express as construct … herself out of the very language used' (Boyle 1997: 31). For ruling-class Romans, their fluency in rhetoric equipped them with a means of public life in politics and the law, and also provided a secure identity in a society where performance was a key means of exercising power.

In Seneca's Stoic philosophy nature embodies a divine and benevolent force. In Seneca's *Phaedra* nature is an amoral and violent force, embodying an irresistible sexual imperative oblivious to human happiness. Rather than the ambivalence and contradiction which often characterises Greek tragedy, in imperial Roman tragedy there is a view of human beings as the playthings of vast and implacable powers. In his opening speech Hippolytus talks of nature as the goddess Diana's empire, a place to be violently plundered, and even ravished: Diana is the 'masculine goddess,/for whose kingdom lie open the secret parts of the earth' (Seneca 2010: 4), and whose boundaries significantly correspond to those of the Roman empire itself (Boyle 1997: 62). In the following ode the chorus talk of the power of Venus, goddess of sexual love, in similar terms to how the realm of Diana, goddess of wild nature was described by Hippolytus – as all-pervading destroyer which takes its vengeance on everyone (11–12). Hippolytus he thinks is the representative of Diana, and when he is about to kill Phaedra he refers to the act as a sacrifice to that goddess. The imperial power of sex pervades the whole world.

But in fact Hippolytus will be Diana's victim. The chorus tell us that Diana herself looks with desire upon the beautiful Hippolytus, 'but seldom has beauty come to men unpunished' (25). When the monster arises from Venus's own realm, the sea, to destroy him, it takes the form of a bull, a symbol of the male sexual desire which Hippolytus has repressed. The wild landscape which he had described in sexual terms at the beginning of the play wreaks sexual violence upon him: 'at last a charred branch from a tree-trunk pierced him/ right in the middle of the groin' (33; Boyle 1997: 66). The chorus conclude that there is some kind of order in the universe: Diana has paid her 'greedy uncle' (Hades) back for Theseus escaping from the realm of the dead (34). In the play's final moments Phaedra's corpse lies unacknowledged on stage as Theseus attempts to piece together the fragments of Hippolytus's corpse. There is an obvious allusion to the end of Euripides' *Bacchae* here (see above, p. 31), where again an all-powerful divine force torments mankind, but there is something more comprehensible in Seneca's depiction of nature, perhaps especially for audiences in the years since Darwin and Freud (see below, p. 118). There is also perhaps a gruesome, macabre comedy in Theseus's concern to solve the puzzle of how to fit the parts of Hippolytus's body together again (37), a howl of bleak laughter against the horror and cruelty of the world, a quality in Seneca which was later to appeal to the sixteenth-century English playwrights who bore his influence.

FURTHER READING

Aeschylus' *Persians* shows the defeat of the Persians by the Athenians at Salamis from the Persian point of view. Sophocles' *Ajax* explores the situation of a war hero hated by a god, whose nature and actions inspire both pity and disgust; *Oedipus at Colonus* completes Oedipus's journey towards death, finding some peace in human compassion at last. Euripides' *Hippolytus* is the first surviving dramatic version of the Phaedra myth; his *Trojan Women* explores the degradations and sufferings of women in war with a stark bleakness; his later plays such as *Alcestis* feature a 'happy' but conflicted ending. Seneca's *Thyestes* expresses the barbarism of his tragic world with gruesome clarity.

Hall (2010) is probably the most comprehensive advanced introduction to Greek tragedy and is especially good at placing the plays in context. Easterling (1997b) remains an invaluable guide to key issues, ideas and debates on Athenian tragic theatre. Segal (1983) contains a very representative selection of twentieth-century criticism. Goldhill (1986) brings the insights of late-twentieth-century literary theory to bear on the genre. There are a number of fine studies of how the plays could work, and still do work in performance: Taplin (1985), Wiles (2000) and Goldhill (2007). For Roman tragedy, Boyle (1997) is a persuasive study of the style, form and content of Seneca's tragedies in their context. Boyle (2006) considers the other Roman tragic writers whose work survives in fragments and the development of genre. Silk (1996) is a more advanced but fascinating collection of essays and responses which debate critical issues in Greek tragedy and its later influence.

2

'WHEN THE BAD BLEED'?

EARLY MODERN ENGLISH TRAGEDY

Theatrical tragedy almost disappeared in the Middle Ages. The term itself came to mean not much more than a cautionary tale for Christians about how the power of the rich and mighty will not last, just like all worldly things. The Latin term often used to describe these 'tragedies' is *de casibus*, meaning 'concerning the falls [of great men]'. Tragedy in English was reinvented as a genre on the London stage at the end of the sixteenth century.

Tragedy seems to flourish when societies are in major transition between different modes of organisation. The French **existentialist** philosopher Albert Camus wrote that 'Tragedy is born in the west each time that the pendulum of civilisation is halfway between a sacred society and a society built around man.' (quoted in Dollimore 1984: 8) This idea could be seen to apply to both classical Athens and sixteenth-century England (but perhaps not so convincingly to the great tragedies written in Catholic Spain in this period by Calderon and Lope de Vega). At this time in England the medieval feudal system was being supplanted by a more centralised political power and by a capitalist economy built on trade and commerce. Coupled with the religious upheavals of the Reformation, these developments produced a change in the way people saw their place in the world, and created a particular need to respond to human suffering at a time when the means of understanding it were widely contested. As in Athens, there also was sufficient wealth for society to sustain a group of writers and an audience with leisure to attend the theatre. These ideas about the right conditions for tragedy to flourish originate with Hegel (see above, p. 24), and in this chapter his approach to tragedy will feature quite often.

If there is one major concern of early modern English tragedy it is justice, both divine and human. Many plays are concerned with suffering that arises from injustice and with its redress, whether human or divine. It is no accident, then, that revenge tragedy is such a dominant form in this period. But there is a key difference here with Greek tragedy. Whereas ancient Athenian tragedy might be often said to be dialectical, setting up opposing ways of understanding a tragic situation for the audience to reflect upon, early modern English tragedy is more interrogative: asking searching questions of its audience about the kind of world its audience lived in, but without pointing to any definite answers.

There is a clear change of mood in the plays written in the reign of Elizabeth I (1558–1603) and James I (and VI of Scotland) (1603–25), and it is useful to split discussion of the period between these two eras.

CONTEXTS: ELIZABETHAN TRAGEDY

There were at least three sets of factors that led to the recreation of tragedy in Elizabethan London. They can be broadly described as cultural, economic and religious. In northern Europe one of the most important cultural developments of the Renaissance period was the growth of Humanism and its establishment in schools and universities. At the heart of this movement was a belief in the power of education to enable each individual to fulfil the potential which God had made possible. Education meant studying ancient Latin and Greek texts to learn both how to write and to argue, but also to derive wisdom and understanding from these renowned authors. Reason was prized above the authority of rulers or even, as it would turn out for some, of the Catholic Church. Roman plays were taught at the grammar schools and universities, both the comedies of Plautus and

Terrence and the tragedies of Seneca (see above, p. 38). Students were also encouraged to take part in the performance of drama in Latin. When, from the 1570s onwards, the need arose for scripts to be performed in London's burgeoning entertainment industry there were plenty of young men educated in classical drama who had learned to think critically about the world around them and who were ready to provide them. For the public stages they did not copy the form and style of Roman tragedy, but developed a new form of theatre with its roots in the popular religious drama traditionally staged by craft guilds, but now being suppressed by Protestantism. The playwright Ben Jonson (1572–1637), who saw himself as the most scholarly of his contemporaries, did try to stay close to the principles of Roman tragedy on the public stage with his *Catiline* (1611), but the play was a flop. Earlier he had also been commercially unsuccessful in a subtle, brilliant and still under-appreciated reworking of classical tragedy with his *Sejanus* (1603) (McEvoy 2008: 43ff). Successful early modern English tragedy sought to go its own way.

By the final years of the sixteenth century London was by far England's biggest city and had become a major trading port as well as a centre for all kinds of industry. It had developed an educated middle class with the money and leisure time to seek entertainment. The first commercial playhouse opened in London in 1574, and many more were to follow. London was a dynamic city with a mobile, rapidly growing population, a high mortality rate and extremes of wealth and poverty. Capitalism and individualism were now clearly emerging as powerful forces out of the feudal, medieval past and the conflict between one rising and one declining ideology was full of tragic potential for individuals. This conflict was played out again and again in the plays of this period. The purpose-built Elizabethan playhouses were built as private, profit-making enterprises in the suburbs, out of the control of the City's ruling council. Here, all-male companies of professional actors performed on raised stages in the open air, surrounded on three sides by standing spectators crammed together in the 'pit'. Those who had paid more for a seat sat in tiered galleries which encircled the pit. At the back of the stage was the 'tiring house' from which the actors generally entered through two or more doors. Above the tiring house was a gallery for musicians, or for use as an upper stage. These public amphitheatres could hold about 2,500 people (Gurr 2009a: 261). Tragedy was played out within touching distance of a tight-packed, attentive audience.

Religion was the most contentious matter in early modern England. In the 1530s King Henry VIII had taken his new Church of England out of the control of the Roman Catholic Church. England became an officially Protestant country (apart from during the brief reign of Henry's daughter Mary), but there were a variety of different forms of Protestantism which flourished at different times. There were still also many people who saw themselves as Catholics. Perhaps the most radical Protestant idea was that each person had an individual and personal relationship with God which required no mediation by the hierarchy of the church. Each person had a connection with an omnipotent power who could damn or save their soul for ever; each individual had the potential for a tragic fate to be endured eternally. Those Protestants who followed the ideas of the Swiss reformer Jean Calvin (1509–64) were particularly strong in London. Calvin had taught that people cannot win salvation through their own actions, but that God only granted heaven to those he had chosen for his own impenetrable reasons: the doctrine of 'double-predestination' proposed that only a minority of the human race would not be damned for all eternity, and there was nothing the individual could do about this apart from look for the signs of God's Grace in their lives and in their hearts which might show that they were one of the 'elect'. Both Catholics and Protestants generally shared the belief in divine **Providence**: the idea that God will reward the good and punish the bad both in this world and the next. This might be regarded as an anti-tragic notion, since it suggests that human suffering is part of a greater, benevolent plan, and that pain and sorrow are either deserved or justifiable. But this notion is interrogated again and again in English tragedy of this period. The most strict Protestants, known popularly as 'Puritans' believed that the whole institution of theatre was ungodly.

The new tragedy that emerged in the 1580s and 1590s preserved the violence and horror of Seneca's work, as well as a love of elaborate rhetoric. There was plenty of classical allusion, and there were even Latin quotations in the plays. The tragic protagonist was typically an individual at odds with the powerful, either mortal or divine, who asserts their own need for vengeance, as in Shakespeare's bloody first tragedy *Titus Andronicus* (1592), or for self-fulfilment, as in the case with Marlowe's two *Tamburlaine* plays (1587–90). The first great and enduringly popular tragedy was Thomas Kyd's *The Spanish Tragedy* (1588?). We know little of Kyd (1558–94), apart from his unfortunate connection with Christopher Marlowe (1564–93). Marlowe, who seems to have been involved in anti-Catholic espionage, street brawling and counterfeiting, was accused of blasphemy in 1593. Incriminating papers were found in the lodgings he had shared with Kyd two years before. Poor Kyd was tortured to extract further information. Marlowe was murdered in dubious circumstances shortly afterwards. It seems that Kyd never recovered from the disgrace and died the following year.

THOMAS KYD, *THE SPANISH TRAGEDY* (1588?) AND REVENGE TRAGEDY

The Spanish Tragedy was written at the time of the Spanish Armada and was still being performed right up to the closure of the London theatres at the beginning of the Civil Wars in 1642 (Gurr 2009b: xviii). The play opens with the ghost of Don Andrea, accompanied by the allegorical figure of Revenge. The pair serve as a chorus at the beginning and end of each act. Both these features recall Senecan tragedy. Andrea has emerged from the classical underworld to observe the vengeance which has been promised on Prince Balthazar of Portugal, who had apparently killed the Spaniard in battle when unhorsed and defenceless (Kyd 2009: 1.4.19–26). Balthazar in turn was captured by Horatio, the son of Spain's Chief Justice, Hieronimo, and the Spanish forces were victorious. To conclude peace between the countries the childless King of Spain plans to marry Balthazar to his niece Bel-Imperia, who had been the lover of the low-born Andrea. To spite these plans Bel-Imperia begins an affair with Horatio, but the pair are discovered and Balthazar and Bel-Imperia's brother Lorenzo stab Horatio and hang him in the arbour where he had held his tryst with Bel-Imperia.

Hieronimo and his wife, Isabella, discover their dead son. He promises revenge. A letter written in Bel-Imperia's blood accuses Balthazar and Lorenzo, but Hieronimo fears it may be a trap and awaits further proof. Another letter discovered on the body of one of their executed accomplices, Pedringano, provides that assurance. Increasingly crazed, Hieronimo seeks justice from the King, but is dismissed as mad. He contemplates suicide, but rejects both that act and also the Christian injunction to leave vengeance to God (3.12.20) and decides to assume a pretend calm (3.12.30). His wife does kill herself in despair. Finally, urged on by Bel-Imperia, he persuades Lorenzo and Horatio to take part in a play alongside himself and Bel-Imperia before the court and the Viceroy of Portugal. Under the cover of the drama he kills his son's murderers and Bel Imperia dies at her own hand. Revealing the body of his dead son to justify himself, he bites out his own tongue before stabbing the King's brother the Duke of Castile and ending his own life, leaving both kingdoms heirless. The ghost of Andrea exults over torments that await his slain enemies in the pagan underworld.

The Spanish Tragedy effectively established a whole genre of early modern plays, the revenge tragedy, which possessed a number or recognisable conventions. The setting for these plays, a corrupt or badly ruled court, is always safely beyond English shores so that no obvious accusation of 'application' could be made against the dramatist or the theatre company. If the authorities felt that a member of the court was being attacked on stage, the consequences could be serious, as Ben Jonson and others found out (McEvoy 2008: 3–4). But the court context ensured that revenge tragedy was always political in its orientation. Hieronimo is also the prototype malcontent, the disaffected avenger who has been alienated from his society because of a perceived lack of justice. Hamlet (see below, p. 54) and Bosola in *The Duchess of Malfi* (see below, p. 80) are generic descendants of Hieronimo. The malcontent and the audience tend to be united in the common knowledge of the concealed crimes committed by the powerful in these plays, and the process of **dramatic irony** often creates a bond which allies the watchers to a man who is committed to vengeful violence. The antagonist of the malcontent is often the '**machiavel**', the cunning and ruthless plotter for whom winning is everything, and morality something to be feigned in the quest for dominance (a popular simplification of the political teachings of the Italian political theorist Niccolò Machiavelli, 1469–1527). Here, the machiavel is Lorenzo; in *Hamlet*, Claudius, and in *The Duchess of Malfi*, the Cardinal.

In *The Spanish Tragedy* events not directly related to the principal action mirror and comment upon the main plot in a kind of montage effect: the Portuguese nobleman Alexandro, who is falsely accused of murdering Balthazar in battle, is condemned to be burnt at the stake. He puts his trust in Heaven, not the corrupt earth (3.1.32–37), as does Hieronimo later. But in Alexandro's case letters arrive proving that Balthazar survives just in time to save his life, and his accuser Villuppo is led away to a violent death. Thus jealousy and deceit is seen to be common in all courts, but Hieronimo's lack of divine help would indicate that providential outcomes may be more accident than divine intervention. When Hieronimo decides that only human action can bring justice he casts aside God's claim that vengeance belongs to him, '*Vindicta mihi*' (3.13.1). But the episode also shows that judgement must not be rushed, again giving credibility to Hieronimo's actions. The use of a performance, game or ritual as a cover for the final slaughter of the guilty (and innocent) is also a common feature of the genre, for example the fencing match at the conclusion of *Hamlet*. But the presence of a play within a play (also a feature of *Hamlet*) has a **metatheatrical** function: it draws attention to the fact that plays have specific impacts upon their audiences and invites reflection on what particular impact this play might be having, perhaps morally and politically. Or alternatively it might simply work to defuse its own moral and political impact by stressing the fictitiousness of the experience of this play.

Critics of the play have focused on the morality of revenge. It is far from clear that Hieronimo is enacting divine justice, especially when he kills the Duke of Castile, the Spanish King's blameless brother at the end. The pagan chorus of Andrea and Revenge then sentences Castile's spirit to eternal torment (4.5.32). Despite Castile's innocence it is upon ruling families that revenge is taken. The critic Linda Woodbridge has proposed that the avengers of these plays, such as Hieronimo, were not (and are still not) seen by their audiences as part of some debate on the nature of divine justice and the workings of providence, but rather are urged on because they are taking retributive action against the gross unfairness of the society they found themselves in. 'Much of *The Spanish Tragedy*'s injustice', she writes, 'is class-inflected' (Woodbridge 2010: 237). Horatio is patronised by the nobles in the play, and his social inferiority is a principal reason why he must be disposed of as Bel-Imperia's lover (3.10.54–57). Lorenzo pointedly jokes about Horatio going up in the world when his murdered body is strung up (2.43.60–61). Neither is Lorenzo concerned that the two 'base companions' who have helped him conceal Horatio's murder should die (3.2.115). Balthazar thinks when he acts in the play at the end that a courtier such as he will be able to tell his inferiors 'how to speak' (4.1.105), 'lines that must have tasted sour to the professional actor who spoke them', as Woodbridge (2010: 238) remarks. She shows how Hieronimo is ignored by the King when he tries to get justice, faced by men 'Who as a wintry storm upon a plain,/Will bear me down with their nobility' (3.13.37–38), as he tells the audience. Rather than consider that there may be some problem with the text, Woodbridge suggests that the reason why the King of Spain still does not understand the killings at the end of the play (4.4.165), despite the long speech Hieronimo has just made explaining himself (4.4.73–152), is that Kyd is showing how the upper class have never listened to complaints of injustice. Woodbridge (2010: 240) writes:

> Upper-crust selective deafness explains why Hieronimo becomes an avenger rather than a legal plaintiff. Upper-class incomprehension reveals why revenge plays appealed to ordinary folk ... a society can habitually be unjust through class inequity. Hieronimo dies, but takes the upper echelons with him, leaving two royal families heirless – satisfying to the frustrated and powerless in the audience.

Revenge tragedy seen in this way can look forward to twentieth-century views of tragedy such as those of Raymond Williams (see below, p. 138): a fractured, unjust society is mirrored on stage where violence is the only means of striving towards some justice – but always at great cost in suffering to both victim and oppressor.

CHRISTOPHER MARLOWE, *DR FAUSTUS* (1588?)

Marlowe based his protagonist on a series of notorious men who had despaired of or had challenged God's power to condemn them to hell, and in particular a German magician called Faustus who was reputed to have sold his soul to the devil (Hopkins 2008: 27). Marlowe's Faustus is an eminent scholar who opens the play bored with the vast knowledge he has accrued through his studies, and turns to magic to gain power, wealth and excitement. He uses necromantic spells to summon up a devil, Mephistopheles, who will obey his commands and answer his questions about the secrets about the universe. But he must enter into a contract, signed with his own blood, to give his soul to the devil after twenty-four years have passed. In return, Mephistopheles will 'do for him and bring him whatsoever' (Marlowe 1995a: 2.1.100). There are two different texts of the play that have come down to us, the A-Text published in 1604, and the longer B-Text published in 1616. How Faustus uses this power in his twenty-four years differs in the two versions, but it is mostly spent in practical jokes, including hitting the Pope over the head whilst he and Mephistopheles are invisible (3.2.87). He does have sex with the summoned-up spirit of Helen of Troy, but otherwise he has little that is heroic or world-conquering to show for twenty-four years of ultimate power. In a series of sub-plot scenes his servant Wagner re-enacts his necromancy to crude and absurd effect, undercutting his master's magical deeds.

It seems as though Faustus had never really believed that his damnation would truly come, even telling Mephistopheles that 'Hell's a fable' (154; 2.1.127). Several times he tries to repent, but either cannot or will not. Calvinist Protestants watching the play would take his inability to repent as proof that he had been damned from the beginning, while those of a more Lutheran persuasion would regard his salvation as still possible if he were granted the Grace to repent (the wording of the A-Text gives a more Calvinist reading of the play, interestingly enough; see above, p. 46) (Hopkins 2008: 31). Finally, time races away from him, and Faustus, in terror, is desperate to escape his fate, but he cannot. The clock strikes and Mephistopheles arrives to drag him down to Hell.

Throughout the play Faustus possesses a wit and charm which belie the hubris and megalomania he exhibits at times. He is a vulnerable and at times childish figure who never really harms anyone. Even the old man who tries to get him to repent, and whom Faustus summons devils to torment, escapes the fiends to reach heaven (5.1.118). Right at the very end, when eternal damnation beckons, he cannot resist showing off his classical learning when inappropriately quoting the Roman poet Ovid and wishing that Pythagoras's doctrine of the transmigration of souls between creatures was true (5.2.66; 5.2.99–101). Since Harry Levin's (1961) study of Marlowe it has been a critical commonplace to regard Marlowe's protagonists as 'over-reachers', heroic individuals who strive to go beyond the limitations of their age, in learning, religion, class and politics. As a tragic figure, Faustus must have seemed to his Christian audience, on the one hand, to have sought his own damnation through his arrogance. But, on the other hand, he possesses an attractive energy and humanity which enables him plausibly to challenge the limits of what is acceptable in a society which was about to go through rapid economic, political and technological change. In this Hegelian sense (see above, pp. 24 and 45) Faustus is tragic because he is a figure caught between two different historical moments: a 'modern', free-thinking, intellectually open and socially ambitious man in a society which is only beginning to shake off its medieval ways of thinking.

We do not know how the original audience reacted to the play (though there is evidence that there was a genuine fear that the magic words used in the play might indeed summon up real devils on stage, so theatrically powerful is the drama; Hopkins 2008: 50–51). Modern audiences at least do not nod sagely at the rightness of Faustus's damnation, and it is hard to believe that this would have been the universal response of spectators and readers in the late sixteenth century.

Faustus is above all a man of books, texts to which he has devoted his life, which are the source of his knowledge, and the root of his power to summon devils. But his contract is not written in ink; it is written in his own blood, and the words which warn him to fly from the devil appear etched onto his own skin (2.1.76–77). The play insists that there is a real life beyond books and plays, a physical life of the body which ages and must die at the end of our own term. Mephistopheles' answer to Faustus's claim that hell is fictional is the chilling 'Ay, think so still, till experience change thy mind' (2.1.128). Only in his last line in the play does Faustus finally offer to burn his books. *Dr Faustus* is also a most theatrical and spectacular of tragedies: there are fireworks, processions of cardinals, a parade of the Seven Deadly Sins, conjuring tricks and both Satan and Helen of Troy appear on stage. All this is flamboyantly stagey, and Faustus cannot really take it seriously much of the time. But Marlowe insists on the distinction between the power of the literary, most evident in stage production (and, by blatant analogy, in religious texts and rituals), and what the twentieth-century tragedian Edward Bond calls 'the world we prove real by dying in it' (Bond 1983: lxvi). In the gap between this exciting, complex and conflicted theatrical and verbal vision of what the world might be and the facts of life as we live it in our mortal bodies lies perhaps the tragedy of Marlowe's play. The great power of the imagination embodied in life and art, for good and ill, is the product of our fragile and impermanent bodies.

The sense of tragedy grows in a frustrating way as the play progresses and Faustus's use of his powers seems to grow more wasteful and more trivial, increasing the sense of futility before Satan's final triumph. But it is important to note that in the eyes of his contemporaries Marlowe was thought of as an atheist (Hopkins 2008: 111–14). Diabolical evil for him is also fictional, merely theatrical and thus man-made, and in that lies some grounds for hope for us.

Postmodern critics of the play, however, ably critiqued by Richard Wilson (2000: 127–8), have argued that, since all language is unstable in meaning and the product of powers beyond our control, the deconstruction and reduction to nothingness of this man composed of books and writing demonstrates that we are no more than the constructs of the language we are born into (see, in relation to this, the box on Jacques Lacan below, p. 159). There is no room for tragedy in such a reductive, ultimately perverse reading which merely finds a shallow 'playfulness' in the workings of language and power.

WILLIAM SHAKESPEARE, *HAMLET* (1600–1601)

When Shakespeare rewrote an earlier, now lost, revenge tragedy about a legendary Danish prince he gave the genre a depth and scope it had never previously achieved. Moreover, he produced what has become probably the most performed play in the history of the theatre.

As the play begins Denmark has a new king. Claudius has just succeeded his brother Old Hamlet and married his queen, Gertrude. Old Hamlet's ghost appears to his distraught son, Hamlet, and reveals that he was murdered by Claudius. The ghost demands that revenge is carried out. Hamlet enjoins those who have also witnessed the ghost to secrecy, and says that he will pretend to be mad. But he delays taking any action against the king. A play is staged by the Prince which re-enacts the ghost's account of the murder, which may or may not provoke a guilty reaction in the King; at any rate the King orders the play to be stopped. Hamlet kills the king's chief minister, Polonius, by mistake, thinking that he was the King secretly overhearing his heated, accusatory exchange with his mother Gertrude. Polonius was also the father of Hamlet's beloved Ophelia, who subsequently goes mad with grief and dies by drowning. The circumstances of Polonius's killing are hushed up and Hamlet is sent to England with covert orders for his own execution. Ophelia's brother Laertes then storms into the palace at the head of a crowd of Danish people demanding revenge, but the King calms him down and persuades him to take part in a plot against Hamlet's life; the prince has returned unexpectedly, having outwitted and destroyed the two old friends who were guarding him. Hamlet agrees to fight a fencing match with Laertes. The bout is a trap laid by the king to take Hamlet's life, but the plot backfires, and the play ends with the deaths of Gertrude, Laertes, Claudius (at Hamlet's hands) and finally of Hamlet himself. Fortinbras, prince of Norway, arrives at the crucial moment and seizes the throne.

The ethics of revenge in a Christian society, when both God and the state claim the right to exact retribution for killing, are at the centre of the play. But Hamlet's dilemma – should he carry out the ghost's command to take vengeance or should he maintain his allegiance to the anointed king? – becomes the setting for the play's remarkable exploration of a series of philosophical and political issues.

To begin with, the ghost is a recognisably Catholic figure, emerging as he does from Purgatory (1.5.11–20), a halfway house between heaven and hell whose existence was denied by Protestants since it is not mentioned in the Bible. Protestantism was of course the state religion of both Shakespeare's England and of contemporary Denmark. The ghost is also a figure from the heroic feudal past when kings fought each other in single combat to settle territorial disputes (1.1.79–94), rather than resorting to diplomacy as the modern Claudius does (1.2.17–41). To this extent Hamlet can be seen as a tragic figure caught between the demands of two conflicting **ideologies**, one declining (the Catholic, feudal warrior-run country) and one rising (the Protestant nation-state with a politician-king). Whatever Hamlet does in response to the ghost's demands he will go against the moral, religious and political demands of one of these two belief-systems, and in this double-bind resides his tragedy.

The final winner is the apparently untroubled military adventurer Prince Fortinbras of Norway, who arrives on stage to find the royal family of Denmark dead before him, having unaccountably strayed from the route he had been granted with his forces to travel through the kingdom (2.2.75–80). In this moment Shakespeare also calls into question the grounds of monarchy itself and its claim to be justified by divine sanction. Earlier, in one of the play's most outrageous pieces of dramatic irony, the murderous usurper Claudius successfully faces down the irate and armed Laertes by asserting that God will always protect the legitimate king, leaving treason to but 'peep to what it would' (4.5.123). We had also just been reminded that the Danish 'rabble' had claimed the right to choose their own king, forgetting 'antiquity' and 'custom' in the matter of who takes power in the land (4.5.100–106). That in Roman antiquity a would-be monarch, Julius Caesar, had been assassinated by republicans defending their country from monarchy has been referred to twice in the play by this point (in a passage in the Second Quarto text, Shakespeare 2006: 1.1.113 and 3.2.99–100). The question of vengeance against a murdering monarch becomes expanded in this play into an examination of the just grounds for monarchy itself (see Hadfield 2005: 184–204).

Perhaps both the monarchy and revenge are kinds of public performances for effect. *Hamlet* is intensely aware of its own status as a play. In order to prove to himself that the ghost is not a devil sent to trick him (2.2.600–605) Hamlet arranges for some actors who are performing at court to re-enact his father's murder just as the ghost told it. He watches Claudius's reactions to this on-stage performance closely to see if they will demonstrate his guilt. Although the King gets to his feet and leaves just after the poisoning is acted out (3.2.253–57), it is notoriously unclear whether he does so out of guilt or mere disgust with Hamlet's antics; Hamlet is convinced, although his friend Horatio is not. Those who justified the theatre against its Puritan critics at the time argued that it taught moral lessons, but here Shakespeare seems to be making the audience reflect on their own response to *Hamlet*, and to cast doubt on whether the theatre can have a clear moral impact at all. In his first substantial speech in the play Hamlet also proclaims that he is feeling a grief which no actor could represent on stage, further undermining the claims of theatre to portray the real world in a meaningful way (1.2.77–86). He also marvels at how an actor can portray a depth of emotion for an imaginary character when he cannot rouse himself to take action against his father's murderer (2.2.552–74). Yet all this only reinforces for the audience Hamlet's own fictional status.

Despite this Hamlet achieves a convincing notion of his own 'interiority': that we have here before us a human consciousness fully laid out in a sympathetic, believable way, a mind which audiences have found it possible to understand and identify with, especially in modern times. Partly this is to do with the frankness and emotional neediness of his soliloquies, partly through the sparkling nature of his wit and the way in which he engages the audience through asides to laugh with him at his opponents, and partly through the range of ideas over which Hamlet's language roams on its long journey through the play. It's plausible to argue that in Hamlet Shakespeare develops a new kind of dramatic protagonist, seldom matched since in its depth, complexity and capacity to involve the spectators. In doing so, the sense of tragic pathos, of emotion felt for the loss of the Prince is greatly enhanced. In this play the idea of a young man constantly forced to confront death in his personal, political and emotional life brings into stark relief a powerful sense of the tragic. Harold Bloom wrote that 'as a meditation upon human fragility in confrontation with death, it competes only with the world's scriptures' (Bloom 2003: 3). But, perhaps unlike in scripture, that meditation never settles on any fixed position, and constantly critiques itself. As the play moves into its second half it is the 'villain' Claudius who addresses the audience confidentially (e.g. 3.1.52–56, 3.3.36–72) taking over from Hamlet, as the Prince's actions become more murderous, cruel and wayward. The King becomes, as Terence Hawkes put it, 'a complex, compelling figure … whose mightiness constantly tugs back recursively, against the smooth flow of the play' (Hawkes 1986: 100).

Hamlet's own inability to settle on a fixed position from which to contemplate human mortality and to answer the questions it asks about the individuals and society it represents – and even its own status as a representation – exist in tension with its thriller-like form and its powerfully effective sequence of set-piece dramatic conflicts. *Hamlet* is a great tragedy, but also possesses so much more in excess of the tragic.

ANDREW BRADLEY AND THE 'TRAGIC FLAW'

A.C. Bradley's book *Shakespearean Tragedy* was first published in 1904 and has been in print ever since. It has exerted a notable influence amongst teachers and students, often indirectly. Bradley's approach can seem strange today. He believed that stage production did not do justice to the plays (Bradley 1991: 170), and always writes about the experience of the reader, not the audience in the theatre. Notoriously, he also writes about the characters of the plays as if they had an existence beyond the words on the page, using the texts as clues to construct their lives and activities in the times when they don't appear on stage, as if they were historical figures.

But in fact Bradley (1851–1935) did not believe that the historical circumstances had much relevance for our understanding of Shakespeare's tragedies. 'Character', a set of determining personal qualities possessed by individuals, was what drove the action of the plays, not chance or fate, let alone larger social forces: 'calamities and **catastrophes** follow inevitably from the deeds of men, and ... the main source of these deeds is character' (29). At the centre of the tragedy, as for Aristotle (see above, p. 14), was the protagonist, a remarkable figure with nobility or greatness of some sort whose fall 'produces a sense of contrast, of the powerlessness of man' (27). But, unlike Aristotle, Bradley felt that Shakespeare's tragedies demonstrated that there is what he called a 'moral order' in the universe. This is not Christian **Providence**, though there is a clear Christian element to his theory. This moral order was on the side of cosmic goodness and was evolving towards a better universe. Its workings were played out in the characters of the tragic protagonists in particular, whose personalities contained 'some marked imperfection or deficit', qualities which are 'in the wide sense of the word, evil, and ... contribute decisively to the conflict and **catastrophe**' (48). In Hamlet, the imperfection is his melancholy; in Othello it is that he is easily deceived and rash in action once his emotions are aroused; in Lear, it is his proneness to anger and wilfulness (109, 176, 260). In striving to rid the world of this evil within itself, the moral order destroys the protagonist, with terrible consequences. Bradley claimed that his idea explained both the sense of waste we get at the end of these plays, but also the mysterious, 'inexplicable appearance of a world travailing for perfection, but bringing to birth, together with glorious good, an evil which it is able to overcome only by self-torture and self-waste' (51). This is why he thought we have some pleasure and a sense of hope at the end of a Shakespeare tragedy.

Bradley had been a student and teacher of Hegel's philosophy and his idea that the world is moving forward in some moral sense at the end of each tragedy owes something to Hegel's views (see above, p. 24). But Bradley thought of Shakespeare's characters as principally existing on some kind of universal plane outside history and location, and this is clearly a weakness in his theory. There is also a Christian element to his thinking: for Christians human salvation is brought about by a perfect being (God) taking on an imperfect human form (Christ), which will destroy him as a means to ultimate good, and there is a clear analogy here.

Bradley's ideas became popularised in a phrase he never used, the 'tragic flaw' in the character of a noble person that will bring about their downfall. Although the idea is naïve in its denial of the fact that texts are written in time and are informed by the dynamic circumstances in which they are written, his work on character might be seen to anticipate those later psychoanalytical theories which locate the source of tragedy in the structures of the human mind (see below, p. 159).

CONTEXTS: JACOBEAN TRAGEDY

'Jacobean' refers to the period 1603–25 when King James I of England and VI of Scotland was on the throne (*Jacobus* is Latin for James). Although there was great relief that when Elizabeth I died without an heir a violent succession struggle did not ensue, and even though James ended the long war with Spain and initially sought harmony between religious factions, he soon lost any aura of being a national saviour. James's view of himself as God's representative on earth soon led to a series of conflicts with parliament, a process which would culminate in civil war under James's son Charles in 1642. The free-spending King was notorious for his promotion of attractive-looking favourites to positions of power, and the implication of the court in a series of scandals soon established the idea of that licentiousness and corruption were to be found at the very highest levels. James's parliamentary opponents were predominantly Calvinist Puritans (see above, p. 46) and it was during this period that Calvin's grim view of human existence was at its most influential in England.

Not all modern historians would endorse such a bleak view of this period, but the idea of corruption and misrule at the top of society spreading disastrously through a whole country is evident in the period's drama, particularly in *King Lear* (see below, p. 67). Revenge Tragedy (see above, p. 48), where a troubled outsider takes personal vengeance for the deeds of corrupt rulers, became a very popular genre during these years, prominent examples being Chapman's *Bussy D'Ambois* (1604) and Middleton and Rowley's *The Changeling* (1622). These plays are often very self-knowing. The fact that many of them were also performed by companies of boys, such as Chapman's *Bussy* and Marston's tragicomic revenge drama *The Malcontent* (1603) suggests that self-conscious artifice was sometimes put in the way of an open tragic response. Early in the King's reign Middleton's *The Revenger's Tragedy* (1606) cynically parodies the genre (and especially *Hamlet*) in an outrageous (and very funny) fashion, at times laughing at the theatricality of the whole idea of divine Providence in a society where justice is in the hands of the unjust. In Middleton's play the avenger Vindice poisons the Duke by tricking him into kissing the envenomed and dressed-up skull of the woman he poisoned. As he dies he makes him watch his own illegitimate son embracing as his lover the Duke's wife. The Duke is unable to speak since Vindice's dagger is in his tongue. Vindice's sadistic cruelty undermines the whole notion of just vengeance, but he tells the audience that 'when the bad bleed, then is the tragedy good' (Middleton 1996: 3.6.205). Self-conscious, sensational spectacle may hold the audience's attention, but the plays can teach no virtue in a society where virtue has fled from its conventionally appropriate source. The Duke's victim was called Gloriana, a name for the departed Queen Elizabeth I.

CLIFFORD LEECH AND LIBERAL HUMANIST TRAGEDY

In the middle of the twentieth century, after witnessing the horrors of two world wars and when facing the constant threat of nuclear war, it became harder to find something consolatory in human suffering. Some critics proclaimed the end of tragedy as a viable art form in the modern world (see for example Jan Kott, p. 71 and George Steiner p. 127 below). The work of the English critic Clifford Leech might be taken as representative of those who sought to maintain the idea of tragedy in a godless and threatening universe at this time. Leech's account of the mood of Jacobean tragedy sounds as if he could be talking of his own period in history:

> we are painfully aware that our capacity to suffer has a breaking-point, that our powers of comprehension are dim. Remnants of old faiths jut out now and then like rocks in a troubled sea, but there is no firm footing on them, and the sea is limitless, the laws of its tides unknown, its winds incalculable. The castaway swims vigorously, scans the encompassing horizon.
>
> (Leech 1950: 86)

Leech's account of Shakespeare's plays locates tragic feeling in the idea of inspirational human dignity in the face of terrible suffering. The universe, he considers, lacks any 'kindly or just disposition of things' (11). Rather than there being any sense of Providence which will reward the virtuous, what divine forces may exist are seen to be absent or hostile to humanity. Whatever evil act is committed, it will in turn bring evil consequences far in excess of the original act, consequences which humans are powerless to stop. Leech regards as 'evil' King Lear's 'indecent' demand of a public statement of love from his daughters (see below, p. 67), and even the Duchess of Malfi's disregard of social hierarchy in marrying her steward Antonio (see below, p. 80).

What raises human suffering to tragedy is the capacity of the tragic protagonist to endure and to become increasingly aware of the pain that is inflicted on him or herself. In balance with this feeling of pity and horror we feel for the sufferer is, however, a sense of pride in that capacity to endure: 'because ... the tragic hero is human, a man [sic] with weakness like our own, we feel not merely admiration but pride: we are proud of our human nature because in such characters it comes to fine flower' (16). In enduring his terrible fate, caused by his own weakness, the tragic protagonist justifies man's existence in the universe.

If we are to identify with the protagonist he or she must not be too different from us, either. In this way Leech's work might be seen as a reworking of Aristotle's ideas (see above, p. 14) for a godless, democratic age, with admiration of the human spirit replacing awe at divine power and the common man replacing the noble hero with greatness of spirit. If anything does mark out a tragic hero such as Hamlet, Lear or Macbeth as exceptional it is 'not so much their capacity for endurance as their sharp sense of their own being' (39). The Shakespearean hero becomes a kind of paragon of liberal individualism, whose individualism and capacity for personal choice (even if flawed) fitted the burgeoning market-consumerist society of the time. These plays, wrote Leech, don't offer 'any coherent "explanation" of the condition of humanity, but rather an extraordinarily subtle fusion of [different, individual] points of view' (72–3).

This rather timid liberal-humanist formulation of tragedy with its acceptance of the unchanging nature of injustice and suffering in the universe was to be rejected by left-wing critics (see below, p. 77). But for Leech, on his formulation, 'tragedy offers us a view of things which aims at comprehensiveness, and thus in its scope resembles the great religions of the east and west' (20).

WILLIAM SHAKESPEARE, *OTHELLO* (1604)

Othello is a Moor, a North African warrior who has become a general in the army of Venice. He has secretly eloped with Desdemona, the daughter of Brabantio, a Venetian nobleman. He has also chosen as his second-in-command Cassio, an officer from Florence, making an enemy of his standard-bearer Iago, who had wanted the position. Brabantio accuses Othello of witchcraft and tries to persuade the Duke to punish Othello for abducting his daughter, but Venice needs Othello to lead its forces against a Turkish attack on Cyprus, and Brabantio's requests are denied. Desdemona successfully pleads to be allowed to accompany her husband to war. In fact a storm destroys the Turkish fleet, but on the island Iago gets to work. He succeeds in getting Cassio demoted following a drunken brawl which he provoked, and then sets out to convince Othello that Cassio is Desdemona's lover. Having placed a handkerchief which was a love-token given by Othello to Desdemona in Cassio's possession, an increasingly emotionally deranged Othello is convinced of her infidelity and swears vengeance. Cassio is wounded in a botched assassination carried out by Iago's dupe Roderigo, but Othello, deaf to Desdemona's protestations of innocence, smothers her with a pillow in their marital bed. Iago's wife Emilia tells Othello that it was she who found the handkerchief and gave it to her husband to use, and Othello realises his mistake. Iago kills Emilia, and Othello commits suicide, leaving Cassio in charge in Cyprus.

Othello is in many ways a domestic tragedy about a disastrous marriage that ends in murder, a major example of a minor genre that included plays like the anonymous *Arden of Faversham* (1592). But Shakespeare turns the story of Othello and Desdemona's relationship into a narrative which has much to say about the power and nature of stories, and about tragedy itself. Even if many twentieth-century critics chose, anachronistically (see Sokol 2008: 113ff) but understandably, to make race the central issue in the play, the substance of their tragedy is their adherence to stories about themselves that have no basis in Venetian society, a culture notorious in early-modern England for self-serving duplicity in matters of the heart and for amoral profit-seeking in matters of business. Right up until his renunciation of his wife's love, Othello's own language depicts him to be a knightly warrior, a heroic royal adventurer of near-legendary status. Desdemona falls in love with him upon hearing the story of the dangers he had endured (1.3.166–67). She, for him, becomes the idealised perfect expression of a knight's lady, so integral to his sense of identity that when convinced of her infidelity he cries out that 'Othello's occupation's gone' (3.3.362), and his shattered self is reconfigured as the barbarous avenger, a role which Iago's language has carefully pre-prepared for him. At times she seems so caught up in the idealised story of their love that she lives in a world where she cannot see the dangers of interfering in military decision making (3.3.41–87), where adultery is hard to believe in (5.1.59–61), and where she dies trying to take the blame for her own murder (5.2.90).

The stories both live by are fundamentally at odds with the hard-nosed political pragmatism of Venice's rulers, and, crucially, with the rhetorical power of Iago. Iago is a man entirely motivated by vengeance, greed and hatred, for whom language is something to be shaped into a weapon, not relished in a narrative by which one can live. One of the remarkable features of the play is Iago's capacity to insinuate himself with an audience to the point where they admire his audacity at the very least. In *Romeo and Juliet* (1595) the young lovers conduct their affair using the language and dramatic conventions of contemporary Italianate love poetry, and their self-sacrifice induces their feuding Veronese families to abandon their feudal grudge. But in *Othello* it is the cynical, masculinist and me-first self-projection of commercial Venice which overcomes the discourse of Romance (in its original literary sense of tales of knights going on quests and winning their ladies' love). Iago's glamour and wit implicates us in this process, but his hard-headed selfish 'realism' turns out to be psychotic (2.1.378–82), and ultimately psychopathic.

Yet there is also something embarrassing and foolish about Othello's behaviour. The play dabbles in comic convention, most notably the overhearing scene (4.1.92–207) which quotes from Shakespeare's earlier comedy *Much Ado About Nothing* (1598–9), where the device is used to prompt repressed love, not murderous hatred (*Much Ado* 2.3.36–232; 3.1.23–116). At a clinching point of Iago's persuasion of Othello, Shakespeare cannot resist a very funny crude play on words. When Othello stumblingly asks whether Cassio lay with his wife, Iago quips 'with her, on her, what you will' (4.1.193). Adultery is often the subject matter of farcical comedy, and the block-headed Othello shares many of the qualities of obsessively jealous comic husbands, such as Corvino in Ben Jonson's great Venetian comedy *Volpone* (1605–6). Sexual jealousy of one kind or another – but often concerned with male control of female sexuality – was a staple of early modern revenge tragedy (for example *The Duchess of Malfi*; see below, p. 80). But in *Othello* it is suggested that it is a topic to be exposed by the strictures of comedy, not sufficient grounds for the murders that end in tragedy (an idea that Shakespeare was to bring to fruition in *The Winter's Tale* (1613)).

Audiences often find the Moor maddeningly obtuse in his inability to see how he is being manipulated. In the last part of the play it is Iago's wife Emilia who speaks the plain truth to Othello, disabusing him of his delusions and saying what many of us have been thinking of him, calling him a 'gull', a 'dolt' (5.2.170), a 'murderous coxcomb' (5.2.240). In a scene just before she has also blown apart the patriarchal assumptions underlying Othello's right to vengeance, not only in asserting the equal rights of women to sexual fulfilment (4.3.85–102), but even more powerfully in pointing out that it is control of the 'world' (4.3.79–81) which enables men to rewrite 'a small vice' (5.1.68) as a terrible crime (see Ryan 2002: 88). Iago's only means of silencing this truth-telling is of course murderous violence. But the source of tragedy becomes relocated in the way power is distributed in society, not in a fault in human nature, nor in a racial characteristic. Compared with *King Lear*, *Othello* is a tragedy on a small scale, but it has much to say about the scope and sources of tragedy in sexual relationships.

WILLIAM HAZLITT: TRAGEDY IS THE 'REFINER OF THE SPECIES'

The English **Romantic** critic and essayist William Hazlitt (1778–1830) was an astute and perceptive writer on Shakespeare's plays in performance. Hazlitt thought Shakespeare the greatest of all dramatists, in as much as only his plays can show us 'the dread abyss of woe in all its ghastly shapes and colours ... laying open all the faculties of the human soul to act, to think and to suffer, in direst extremities' (Hazlitt 1857: 33). He even claimed that Shakespeare's ability to represent 'the greatest heights and depth of action and suffering' was 'on a par with' Nature itself (Hazlitt 1857: 32–3). But for Hazlitt Shakespeare's greatness was a moral achievement, for tragedy itself has a moral function.

When we watch a great tragedy, wrote Hazlitt, our feelings are excited by seeing powerful emotions and we feel sympathy with the extreme suffering of the characters. This brought about two moral benefits for the audience. Firstly, the power of the art makes us see that the needs of other people are as worthy of attention as our own needs; tragedy 'substitutes imaginary sympathy for mere selfishness', and thus 'it makes a man partaker with his kind' and 'leaves nothing indifferent to us that can affect our common nature' (Hazlitt 1906: 32). But it also makes us see that the excesses of our passions can lead to fatal results. In this way 'tragedy purifies the affection by terror and pity' and 'creates a balance of the affections [emotions]. It makes us thoughtful spectators in the lists [i.e. contests, challenges] of life. It is the refiner of the species' (Hazlitt 1906: 32). *Othello* in particular 'has a closer application to the concerns of human life' (Hazlitt 1906: 32) than any other of his plays.

Hazlitt's ideas on tragedy clearly have their origins in Aristotle's (see above, p. 14), but they are distinctive in suggesting that tragedy is a means of asserting our common humanity. Hazlitt was an admirer of the egalitarian principles of the French Revolution, which began in 1789. It is not the nobility of the tragic protagonist that is significant, as it was for Aristotle, but rather the capacity of tragedy to show us in beautiful form the extremes of suffering to which people are subject. The nobility lies in the 'high and permanent interest' it provides 'beyond ourselves, in humanity as such' (Hazlitt 1906: 32). Hazlitt's view would perhaps explain the pleasure we can feel when watching tragedy as the excitement of warm, positive feelings about humankind in general, and the sense that we are learning to become better people. But sadly there is no evidence that those who have watched the most Shakespearean tragedy are actually the most sympathetic and humane human beings.

WILLIAM SHAKESPEARE, *KING LEAR* (1605–6 AND 1610)

In *King Lear* Shakespeare took English tragedy into new territory, expanding its scope and ambition to express an epic vision of human suffering as both the product of the political arrangements in which we live and as an aspect of the natural world we share together. But he also presents a universe in which the divine seems chillingly and perhaps provocatively absent.

The story of Lear, a mythical pre-Roman British king, had been the subject matter of an earlier play (*c.* 1592) in which Shakespeare may have acted. But he startlingly transformed the story in his own versions (he wrote *The History of King Lear* in 1604–5 and revised his script as *The Tragedy of King Lear*, which was written about 1610 but not published until 1623; some editions conflate the two into a single text but I refer here to the *Tragedy*, one of the two separate versions printed in *The Oxford Shakespeare*). The opening presents a fairy-tale motif (see Belsey 2007: 42–6): the aged Lear wishes to resign his kingship and divide his land between his three daughters and asks each of them to express how much they love him in order to be rewarded with territory. The two eldest, Goneril and Regan, each make elaborate protestations of their love, but the youngest, Cordelia, refuses to play along and says she can say 'nothing' (1.1.88). She sees her sisters' language and disingenuous rhetoric as equating love and property in a manner she cannot accept (1.1.95–103; 223–26). Lear is furious, and banishes her without a dowry. In these circumstances she is rejected by one suitor, the Duke of Burgundy, but accepted by another, the King of France. Britain is divided, between Goneril and her husband Albany, and Regan and her husband Cornwall. Lear thinks he can now spend his time hunting with a hundred riotous knights and staying with his two daughters, but both of them reject him, and the King, whose sanity begins to crumble, is cast out onto the heath in a thunderstorm. Lear's exclusion takes place at the house of the Duke of Gloucester, a nobleman who has been deceived by his illegitimate son Edmond into thinking that his legitimate son Edgar was trying to kill him. Edgar has fled and disguised himself as a madman, 'Poor Tom'. He joins Lear on the heath, who is also accompanied by his Fool and by Kent, a nobleman who had been banished when he stayed loyal to Cordelia and is now also in disguise as Lear's servant Caius. Gloucester is shocked at the King's treatment and helps him get to safety. Edmond tells Regan and Cornwall that Gloucester is conspiring with Cordelia and France, and in retaliation they blind Gloucester and set him also on the heath. Appalled at this act, a servant mortally wounds Cornwall before being killed himself. Edmond becomes Duke of Gloucester and the object of the affections of both Goneril and Regan. Cordelia and a French army now land, and Lear makes his way to Dover where he is tended for and seems to regain some of his sanity. Though they had seemed on the verge of fighting each other, the armies of Goneril and Regan join forces to defeat the French. Cordelia and Lear are taken prisoner, but Edgar, in disguise, kills Edmond in single combat. Goneril, who had poisoned Regan in her attempt to become Edmond's sole lover, kills herself in despair. Dying, Edmond reveals he has ordered the execution of Cordelia and the King, and urges someone to be sent to prevent this. The messenger comes too late to save Cordelia, and Lear arrives on stage carrying her body, then dies broken-hearted. No one is left who will rule a Britain whose people are poor and whose ruling dynasty has destroyed itself.

A useful way of understanding Shakespearean tragedy, as we have seen, is to see its protagonist as caught in a Hegelian struggle (see above, p. 24) between two different clashing historical forces, one declining, one rising, as we saw in *Hamlet* (see above, p. 24) and will see in *Antony and Cleopatra* (see below, p. 74). But Shakespeare goes much further than this in *King Lear*. Edmond, Goneril, Regan and Cornwall do indeed represent the rising, hard-headed individualists for whom custom and tradition, even law must bow to the will to power: as Goneril says of her sister's murder 'the laws are mine … /Who can arraign me for't?' (5.3.149–50). Regan and Cornwall are cruel and sadistic, and the scheming Edmond, who has an Iago-like energy and even some rapport with the audience, dies trying to do good (5.3.218–19). The individualists are shown as evil and worthy of their defeat and destruction. But the traditional forces of feudal monarchy in the play are also shown as worthless. Lear's feudal confusion of love, power and property, which causes him to make his initial error of judgement, is underscored when he sees that once he has no power or property two of his daughters no longer love him. To make political power a function of family relations is a recipe for civil strife, a lesson Britain was eventually to take heed of in the century after Shakespeare died. Kent's dogged feudal loyalty may be admirable in a sense, but it gains no reward and leads only to him following his master to the grave (5.3.297–8). Both forces are discredited and at the end of the play Albany can only, absurdly, propose dividing the kingdom up once more between Kent and Edgar. This suggestion is rejected and Edgar merely insists that they must 'speak what we feel, not what we ought to say' (5.3.299–300).

In giving the play this apparently nihilistic ending Shakespeare was deliberately changing the original legend, and the conclusion to the earlier play, where Cordelia survives and Lear is restored to the throne. His ending so offended the sensitivities of later audiences that Nahum Tate's 1681 version, where Lear survives and Cordelia marries Edgar, was the one performed on the English and Irish stage up until 1756, and carried on being played into the nineteenth century (Tate 1997). In Shakespeare's play there is no sense that order has been restored now that evil is defeated, in accordance with the straightforward conservative view that Shakespeare's tragedies are warnings against disturbing the *status quo*. The storm that rages on the heath is not nature sympathetically reflecting the damage to the 'natural' political order caused by children turning against their parents and subjects turning against their monarch. Instead it shows the indifference of nature to humans and their lives, and it is a means by which Lear discovers what he could not when a king: how miserable are the lives of those who have inadequate means to life in comfort and dignity in this world, and that wealth must be redistributed (3.2.33–6), a lesson Gloucester also learns (4.1.61–4). Lear also learns that political power is not divinely ordained, and that justice itself in his world is too often what serves the interest of the wealthy (4.5.146–51). But, like Edmond, he also knows that 'none does offend, none' (4.5.164), since 'men/ Are as the time is' (5.3.30–31). *King Lear* shows how the way a society is organised in a particular time can establish a set of values, or even conflicting sets of values, which can reduce it to rubble and chaos without there being any divine providence to save it. There is effective virtue and goodness in the world of the play, but it is in the actions of nameless and powerless lower-class characters: Cornwall's servant who tries to stop Gloucester's blinding, giving his life in the process but killing his wicked master (3.7.70–80), and the Old Man, Gloucester's ex-tenant, who helps him in his need, even letting him have his own best clothes (4.1.49–50). It is up to us, as fragile humans, to produce justice and fairness – 'speak what we feel not what we [conventionally, **ideologically**] ought to say'. That is why the play's apocalyptic ending was unacceptable to the **neoclassical** theatre.

The idea of apocalypse, of a world-ending final judgement is clearly alluded to when a trumpet blows (as the Bible foretells will happen at the Last Judgement, Matthew 24:31) before the avenging son, in this case, Edgar, comes to judge (5.3.106–7), and in the speeches of Kent and Edgar (5.3.238–9). The play calls attention to its own epic and mythic status in its reference both to folk-tales and the Bible. But it also underlines its own status as a piece of storytelling in the distressing scene where Edgar convinces Gloucester that he has survived his intended suicide-jump over the cliff-edge at Dover, when the audience can see that he has merely fallen face-down onto the stage (4.5.30–78). Edgar sets up an illusion he hopes will 'cure' his father's despair, and it seems to work (4.5.75–7). *King Lear* itself is a piece of fiction which ultimately encourages us not to despair in the face of an unjust world where there is no divine **Providence**. The play's pre-Christian setting allows Shakespeare to get away with such a position in a time when the theatre was subject to government censorship. Judgement is what the play asks of us at the end: like Lear, it takes experience to open our eyes, and, like the blind Gloucester, to 'see feelingly' (4.5.145) the needs of others; and to accept our shared humanity, no matter what our social rank, as Lear comes to see on the heath (3.2.67–72; 3.4.26–36; 96–102). Lear alone of Shakespeare's tragic heroes dies pointing away from himself and his own sufferings (5.3.287) (Fernie 2002: 206–7). *King Lear* is of course the story of the fall of a noble ruler, but it elevates tragedy once more to a place where it can ask its audience the most challenging questions about the world in which they live.

JAN KOTT AND POST-TRAGIC SHAKESPEARE

In 1964 the Polish academic Jan Kott (1914–2001) published *Shakespeare Our Contemporary (Szkice o Szekspirze)*. The book had an immediate impact on attitudes to Shakespearean production, especially with influential directors such Peter Brook and John Barton. Kott had fought heroically against the Nazi invasion and brutal occupation of Poland during the Second World War and had witnessed terrible events. After the war he was an active supporter of the communist government but later defected to America during the Cold War.

Kott did not read Shakespeare as a writer from the past but as a dramatist depicting the world Kott recognised in his own time. *Hamlet*, for example, with its spies and secret surveillance, seemed all too reminiscent of modern police states (Kott 1964: 50–51). He could 'easily visualise' the Prince 'in black sweater and blue jeans', reading a book (at 2.2.170 stage direction) 'by Sartre, Camus or Kafka', **existentialist** and absurdist writers from the twentieth century (58). 'Absurdism' was a movement in post-war European theatre which depicted human life as random and meaningless, as a kind of sardonic comedy. In a world where God was no longer present, and where faith in the 'progress' of human history had been shattered both by the horrors of the 1940s (the Nazi death camps, atomic weapons) and by communism's deterioration into Stalinist tyranny, tragedy made no sense anymore; human suffering was merely ridiculous. When 'there is no appeal to God, Nature or History from the tortures inflicted by the cruel world,' wrote Kott, 'the clown becomes a central figure in the theatre' (113). Kott thought that the idea of tragedy relied on the 'absolute': something beyond immediate human experience which makes suffering appear inevitable but rational in some cosmic sense. Once the absolute was gone suffering simply appears 'grotesque' – ugly, absurd and crudely comic. Tragedy, on his definition was no longer possible.

Kott's ideas were applied with particular appositeness to *King Lear*, a play which he found to share a common sense of the grotesque with the work of the twentieth-century Irish playwright Samuel Beckett. As a particular example, Kott takes the scene in *King Lear* where the blind Gloucester, led by his disguised son Edgar to what he thinks is the edge of the cliff at Dover, attempts to commit suicide by throwing himself over the precipice (see above, p. 70). The actor performs his supposed fall. In reality he is on flat ground, and Edgar next adopts the disguise of a local man who tells him he saw him fall a long way down but has miraculously survived (*The Tragedy of King Lear*, 4.5.34–80). This is not a tragic representation of human despair, but a kind of theatrical trick, whose meaning lies in a joke which relies on 'the paradox of pure theatre' (Kott 1964: 117); that what we see on stage exists and does not exist at the same time. It's a cruelly funny joke played on a character, but it doesn't matter, since we know that what we're seeing isn't real anyway. In a play in which 'both the medieval and renaissance orders of established values disintegrate' (118; see also above, p. 43) suffering becomes meaningless and its enactment on stage becomes nothing more than the sort of grotesque but unbelievable comic violence of clowns. This:

> pantomime performed by actors on the stage is grotesque, and has something of a circus about it. The blind Gloucester

who has climbed a non-existent height and fallen over on flat boards, is a clown. A philosophical buffoonery has been performed, of the sort found in modern theatre.

(Kott 1964: 119)

Kott's example from 'modern theatre' is from Beckett's *Act Without Words*, a coda to his play *Endgame*, in whose final moments a man performs a comparable physical routine (Beckett 1958: 89).

Kott goes on (Kott 1964: 122) to cite the bleak vision of human life given by Pozzo in Beckett's *Waiting for Godot*: 'one day I went blind, one day we'll go deaf, one day we were born, one day we shall die ... They give birth astride of a grave, the light gleams for an instant, then it's night once more.' (Beckett 1956: 89; see below, p. 135). He says this is the same view as that offered by Edgar to Gloucester in Shakespeare's play:

> Men must endure
> Their going hence even as their coming hither.
> Ripeness is all. Come on.
> (*The Tragedy of King Lear*, 5.2.9–11)

Whether this is Shakespeare's view (as Kott claims) or not, Edgar clearly means something different from Pozzo, seeing human life as part of a **Providential** plan where death comes at the appropriate time for each person (Shakespeare 1992: 243). Kott claims that tragedy has lost its meaning without God to give purpose to human suffering and death. But such a view still recognises the need for a guiding divine presence in the universe, even if it is not there anymore. It is the absence of God, or of the Hegelian sense of inevitable human progress (see above, p. 24) (which was also part of Stalinist Marxism–Leninism), which makes tragedy for Kott an empty category. But the need for a God still haunts and underlies this view of human life. This seems to be a reductive and narrow definition of tragedy. It is perfectly possible to be an atheist and a non-communist and to

> recognise a sense of tragedy in art and in the world. Kott was among the first contemporary theorists of the 'post-tragic' to assert that the concept of tragedy relies upon the existence of something we have now lost, a transcendent 'absolute' outside human experience, to have any meaning. But the very idea of the transcendent absolute remains necessary to the sense of this idea, and indeed makes the condition of the post-tragic paradoxically a tragic one, haunted by loss and grief.

WILLIAM SHAKESPEARE, *ANTONY AND CLEOPATRA* (1606)

When Shakespeare turned to the story of two of antiquity's most notorious lovers as told by the Greek historian Plutarch he found material for a profound tragedy of a different kind. *Antony and Cleopatra* makes us ponder the gap between our deepest feelings about who we are and how we understand ourselves as people, and the way that we are seen and understood by the world at large and its values and narratives. There is a kind of Lacanian sense of loss at being in the world at large in this play (see below, p. 159), explored through the love story of two larger-than-life heroic celebrities of the classical world.

Having overcome the republican assassins of Julius Caesar, three men rule the Roman Empire: Mark Antony, Caesar's great-nephew and adopted son Octavius Caesar and the ineffectual Lepidus. Caesar resents his rival and colleague neglecting his responsibilities whilst Antony indulges his love for the tempestuous and unpredictable Cleopatra, Queen of Egypt. Matters are made worse when Antony's wife Fulvia and his brother wage civil war in Italy. Faced with news of a more threatening rebellion led by Pompey and his pirate fleet, Antony departs from Egypt. Antony swallows his pride in coming to a reconciliation with his younger and more politically astute rival. Fulvia has died, and Antony agrees to marry Caesar's sister Octavia to cement their renewed alliance. Peace is then also made with Pompey, who is later disposed of. Cleopatra is furious at the news of the marriage, beating and threatening the messenger, but Antony is soon back in Egypt again, proclaiming his sons kings of different Roman provinces and allying himself with neighbouring kingdoms. The abandonment of Octavia brings a new hostility between Caesar and Antony (Lepidus has quietly been disposed of by Octavius), and Antony's actions make war certain. Against all sound advice Antony takes on his enemy at sea, and flees ignominiously when Cleopatra panics. Many of Antony's officers defect with their forces to Caesar, but back in Egypt Antony wins one last victory in a skirmish with Caesar before his final defeat. Cleopatra has already enraged Antony by kissing the hand of a messenger from Caesar who sought to detach her from him, but now he blames her for her forces' surrender, and she retires to her family mausoleum, sending a servant to tell Antony that she is dead, in order to test his reaction. In fact he resolves on suicide so he may join her in the underworld. He botches the act, but is carried to the mausoleum where, reconciled to his lover, he dies in Cleopatra's arms. When she discovers that Caesar's kind promises to her are false, and that he intends to parade her in shame in his victory procession in Rome, she and her maidservants kill themselves by the aid of poisonous snakes.

Antony and Cleopatra is Shakespeare's most epic play. The action ranges across continents, but the conflict between Rome and Egypt is more than geopolitical. In the play Rome, personified in the dour Octavius Caesar, stands generally for duty, manliness, the worthiness of political ambition and worldly reputation. Egypt, particularly as represented by the unpredictable and passionate Cleopatra, stands for pleasure, sensual indulgence, the erotic and fulfilments not to be measured in worldly terms. Shakespeare underscores this conflict by embedding in the poetry and the plot a complex pattern of contrasting imagery and motifs, with the solid element of earth expressing Roman qualities, and untrustworthy and fluid water expressing Egypt and its values; see, for example, 1.1.35–38. Antony's disastrous decision at Actium to follow Cleopatra's advice and fight at sea (3.7.28–48), not on the land, is part of this structural pattern in the play.

Caught in the middle of these two irreconcilable figures is Antony. The historical late-republican Roman warlord Marcus Antonius had become one of great heroic figures of classical history in Shakespeare's time, but in this play Antony is an ageing, insecure leader who knows his powers are in decline, and is reliant on his past reputation. He makes a series of blunders, both personal and political, such as marrying Caesar's sister Octavia and then abandoning her. In the second half of the play he keeps calling for more wine just to keep going (3.13.193; 4.2.21; 4.9.34–5; 4.16.44). Even his suicide is bungled. There is something embarrassing about the gap between the legend of Antony and how he appears on stage. Shakespeare's portrayal of another legendary figure, Cleopatra, is even more remarkable. She belittles Antony publicly, provokes him beyond endurance, undermines him as a military commander, and, in defeat, appears to be on the point of betraying him to Octavius Caesar (3.13.60–62). Yet the poetry of the play invests her, and her love for Antony, with a tragic dignity which her actions in the play alone will not sustain. Antony's lieutenant Enobarbus's description of Cleopatra when she first meets her lover on the river Cydnus expresses her paradoxical erotic powers and suggests a deeper nature (2.2.198–233), a more profound meaning to her love than she can express in her own actions. In her great speeches about her lover after his death (4.16.61–90; 5.2.75–99), Cleopatra herself performs a similar service for Antony and for her feelings for him, where poetic description provides a tragic grandeur that their own actions – with the exception of her suicide – cannot provide.

It is easy to see in Antony a figure in some respects like Hamlet (see above, p. 48), tragically caught between two conflicting demands in a moment of historical change: Antony the outdated chivalric warrior thinks he can solve everything by taking on Caesar in single combat (4.1.3–6), but in Octavian he is facing a 'modern' **machiavel** for whom political cunning will always trump knightly valour. That element to the tragedy is certainly there. But, in making such legendary figures the protagonists of his play, and depicting them in this way, Shakespeare puts forward a tragic division for his principals between an individual life as really lived, with all its inconsistencies, failings and contradictions, and the public perception of the 'great'. Beyond that the play suggests that it is poetry, and art itself, which can propose an idea of the self, and an idea of love which real life cannot match, but yet which inspires and gives shape to our sense of self and to our most profound feelings. That idea, which is central to the play, offers a tragic view of human experience and yet an inspiring one; one which validates the art form of tragic drama itself. But, if in the end even Cleopatra's poetry seems insubstantial, and art alone is not enough, it might alternatively hint that there is an inevitable sense of loss between the world as experienced in the language and signifying system into which we are born, and our own subconscious sense of self.

Many in Shakespeare's original audience would have known that final victory of Octavius Caesar would bring an end to a century of civil war in the Roman world, and that in the universal peace under the emperor Augustus (the title Octavian would adopt), Christ would be born and the Christian era begin. But in this most unchristian of plays there is no story of sin and redemption, only a tragedy rooted in the conflict between the messiness of real life and the beauty of the means through which we seek to come to terms with that painful state.

TRAGEDY AND TIME: JONATHAN DOLLIMORE AND KIERNAN RYAN

In the final decades of the twentieth century there was a reaction against the kind of earlier criticism which found in early-modern tragedy a universal notion of the noble or uplifting helplessness of human beings in the face of suffering and cruelty (see, for example, the ideas of Andrew Bradley, p. 57 above, and Clifford Leech, p. 61 above). Instead, many critics sought to find contradictions and difficulties in the plays which they argued could not be smoothed over by some overarching notion of human nature or of the human condition outside time. In particular, they sought to locate the plays securely in the time they were situated – and in the time in which they were being performed and read.

In 1984 Jonathan Dollimore published a controversial but very influential study of Jacobean drama, *Radical Tragedy*. Dollimore suggested that the tragedy of the Jacobean period was instrumental in undermining the dominant ideas of the ruling institutions in England and was part of the process that led to the Civil Wars which broke out in 1642. Not only did the plays subtly challenge orthodox religious belief; they also exposed the true nature of power relations in the country by revealing that the dominant narratives by which the rulers justified their power were just that: stories. The ruling classes and their institutions were presented with a 'theatre in which they and their ideological legitimation were subjected to sceptical, interrogative and subversive representations' (Dollimore 1984: 4). The plays show people constructed by their society and by power imbalances constitutive of that society, not as part of some divine, providentialist plan: 'Jacobean tragedy inscribes social process in – or rather as – subjective identity' (19).

In the first scene of Shakespeare's *King Lear* (see above, p. 61), Dollimore writes, Cordelia's transgression is not a lack of kindness to her father, 'but speaking in a way which threatens to show too clearly how the laws of human kindness operate in the service of property, contractual and power relations' (198). She will not take part in a ceremony where love and property ownership are put in the same scale, revealing how kinship itself is created by the processes in which property is transferred. The character of Edmond the bastard, in his first soliloquy, has a powerful insight into the arbitrariness of inheritance depending on legitimacy (*King Lear* 1.2.1–22), although he draws no radical conclusion from this. Neither does Lear's identification with the poor and wretched suggest that all we need are sympathetic kings. It is only when social breakdown comes that a king can discover the true condition of his subjects: 'to wait for shared experience to generate justice is to leave it too late' (Dollimore 1984: 192). Dollimore underlines the play's refusal to end in a conventional way, where justice seems to have been done and the way ahead is clear. When society collapses in civil war, values collapse too: they don't exist separate from the power structures of society.

Dollimore's argument, even though it precisely situates the plays at their moment of creation in early seventeenth-century England, no doubt also expressed a desire to bring the same scrutiny to the dominant ideology at a moment of political crisis in late twentieth-century Britain. When Kiernan Ryan first published his book *Shakespeare* five years later (Ryan 2002) he explicitly rejected the idea that the plays should just be read in their original context. Ryan's radical idea was that the tragedies should rather be understood in terms of what they disclose about the future – even the times yet to come. To read a text merely as evidence of what was happening in the society that produced it is to treat it as a dead piece of historical evidence, not a living work of art. The present, and the future, have grown out of the past, and works of art such as Shakespeare's tragedies have been influential in creating the world we live in now and in the future. What makes Shakespeare's protagonists tragic, Ryan argues, is that their actions look towards a world (perhaps still in the future) in which their sufferings would be not arise; but the tragic protagonists are of course determined by the structures of their society, in a time when oppressions which we can see as unjust are regarded as 'natural': that is what makes their situation tragic. They are 'citizens of an anticipated age whose values their suffering discloses, pointing us towards more desirable storylines as yet to be scripted by history. Their tragedy is to find themselves ... marooned in a hostile, alien reality which has already contaminated their hearts and minds, and eventually crushes them completely' (Ryan 2002: 72). Human experience isn't uniform over time, as the humanist critics say, and to say so 'drains the tragedies of their power to expose the alterable causes of injustice, violence and despair, and expand our awareness of alternative fates hovering in the wings of what happens' (71).

For Ryan, there is no mystery to Hamlet's puzzling failure to live up to the honour code of his father or his duty to the King (see above, p. 54). Hamlet recognises that 'Denmark's a prison' (2.2.246) and that 'the time is out of joint' (1.5.189). The play is in fact 'the tragedy of having to live and die on the "rotten" (1.4.67) terms of such a place at all, despite the knowledge that life could and should be otherwise, that human beings are not forever doomed to become the scoundrels, pawns and parasites that this sort of society moulds them into' (70). In *Othello*, Emilia's speech in which she exposes the double standard applied to the sexual behaviour of men and women (4.3.83–102; see above p. 65) 'invites us to recognise that the true sexual tragedy springs from Othello's thraldom to the male version of marital jealousy and the male presumption of dominion and possession of which such jealousy is the outcome' (88). Ryan's view of history is one moving towards human liberation from injustice and inequality. Shakespeare's tragedies contain in solution the values of that future that we can now see: they are tragic because their protagonists live by, or are forced to live by, outmoded, unjust values which we see can beyond.

JOHN WEBSTER, *THE DUCHESS OF MALFI* (1613–14)

Webster wrote relatively few plays, perhaps because he was also very busy in the family coach-making business, but this reworking of the life-story of the sixteenth-century Italian aristocrat Giovanna D'Aragona is one of the most remarkable revenge tragedies of the period. The play's Duchess is a beautiful young widow who secretly weds her steward Antonio, despite the warnings of her two brothers not to remarry. Her elder brother is the subtle and wicked Cardinal; her twin brother, Ferdinand, Duke of Calabria, is vain, excitable and clearly harbours incestuous feelings for his sister. The Cardinal places the melancholy ex-soldier Bosola in the Duchess's household as a spy, but she has three children by Antonio before the identity of her husband is revealed to her brothers. Having been surprised in her chamber by the creepy, vicious and vengeful Ferdinand she exiles Antonio on the pretence that he has defrauded her.

They rendezvous at a religious shrine at Ancona, but are banished thence through the Cardinal's power. They separate for mutual safety, but Bosola soon arrests and imprisons the Duchess. Ferdinand then torments her, giving her a dead man's hand to kiss in the dark and showing her a waxwork effigy of what appears to be the corpses of Antonio and her eldest son. A group of madmen then dance around her before the disguised Bosola brings in her coffin and the cords which are used to strangle her. Throughout her torments the Duchess preserves a calm dignity and thinks of her children's welfare – who are killed soon after with her maid. Bosola shows grief at what he has done and admiration for the Duchess, and plans to take vengeance on the brothers. But Antonio returns, ignorant of his wife's fate, and foolishly tries to effect a secret meeting with the Cardinal to see if a reconciliation is possible. But he is mistakenly killed in the dark by Bosola, who then does kill the Cardinal and Ferdinand, but not before he has been mortally wounded by the deranged Duke who in his grief for his sister thinks he has become a wolf. Of the whole family only the Duchess's eldest son remains, who is now proclaimed heir.

The Duchess of Malfi has been perhaps the most performed and highly esteemed non-Shakespearean tragedy from this period, even if, as the critic T. S. Eliot famously put it in 1924, the play provides 'an interesting example of a very great literary and dramatic genius directed towards chaos' (Eliot 1999: 117). In the world of the play evil and cruelty seems to dominate. Even as it consumes itself in the chaotic and random killings of the play's final moments, the rather token presence of the young new Duke at the end is overshadowed by the attentions of Delio, whom we know to be as venal and lustful as the other characters in the play (Webster 2009: 2.4.57–76). At the centre remains the figure of the Duchess, an unambiguous figure of goodness whose love of life, faithfulness and fortitude in the face of horror and death shine out, but whose virtue is powerless against the perverted cruelty of her brothers.

Yet the play is so aware of its own theatricality that it does not so much depict a world as self-consciously play out a series of tragic stage-actions, which suggest that it is the shaping of depicted suffering into art which Webster offers us, rather than any comment on real human cruelty and misery. Twice in the play characters explicitly compare their actions to what they have seen on stage (4.2.277–9 and 5.5.93–4), and the Duchess's torments are also overtly theatrical. The incident with the severed hand (4.1.42–52) and the waxwork display of the pretend corpses of her husband and children (4.1.55–63) are carefully staged pieces of illusion to produce an emotional impact on an audience, like the play itself, but the long scene (4.2) which leads to the Duchess's murder also takes the form of a masque, a staged court entertainment of the time where a group of grotesque dancers would be driven from the stage by the intercession of nobles who would then hymn the divinely inspired qualities of the monarch. In this case the dancing madmen are driven from the stage by Bosola and the executioners, and the central figure is, as Leah Marcus puts it, 'not apotheosized but extinguished' (Marcus 2009: 28). Marcus thinks that Webster is almost embarrassed by the sensationalist means by which he engages his audience, coming close to endorsing the anti-theatrical views of contemporary Puritans as he implicates the audience in the guilty pleasure of nasty spectacle, showing the hollow nature of such grisly display and taking a swipe at the showiness of Catholic rituals of worship (Webster 2009: 41).

It could rather be argued that the success of the tragedy lies in Webster's skill to shape plot and spectacle into a pleasing symmetry which gives order to a world which is a 'mere pit of darkness' (5.5.99), where 'we are merely the stars' tennis balls, struck and banded/ Which way please them' (5.4.53–54). In the 1940s Una Ellis-Fermor argued that the perfection of form in certain tragedies represents forces of righteousness absent in the plays' content and thus offers some sense of moral **catharsis** for the audience (Ellis-Fermor 1945: 133). This would unconvincingly suggest that there is some inherent moral quality in well-shaped works of art. It might be more plausible to argue that, like all tragedies, the play seeks to make some sense of inhumanity and cruelty but does so by turning these things into self-consciously fictional spectacle (the sensationalism is part of the guilty pleasure, but it is a pleasure because we know it isn't real). Webster's tragedy is a closed system of self-referential signs; it has given up on representing a world so vile and meaningless that it can only gesture towards it in a series of self-consciously gripping theatrical displays. And yet it also offers a beguiling stage version of beauty and virtue in the character of the Duchess. For Webster, tragedy is a kind of guilty playing with artfully depicted human suffering, but the equally artfully achieved guilt acknowledges that we could perhaps be doing much more about cruelty and prejudice towards the innocent.

The artistic self-consciousness which developed in Jacobean tragedy was a sign of the genre losing its stark power, and towards the end of James's reign, and under Charles, tragicomedy, with its assured happy ending, became the more dominant kind of play. The London theatres were closed when the city was under Puritan control during the Civil Wars and the Commonwealth (1642–60). When tragedy returned to the English stage it would be in a very different form.

FURTHER READING

Several plays to extend your reading of early modern tragedy are mentioned in the text. Marlowe's *Tamburlaine the Great* shows a conqueror of boundless ambition (and cruelty) taking on God himself (Marlowe 1995b). Shakespeare's *Titus Andronicus* is a shocking reworking of Senecan tragedy with much to say about politics. His late tragedy *Coriolanus* also examines the role of the military leader in conflict with popular politics in a Roman setting. Another Roman play, Ben Jonson's *Sejanus, His Fall* is a far more subtle reworking of classical tragedy than neoclassical authors managed (Jonson 1990). Middleton and Rowley's *The Changeling* (Middleton and Rowley 2007) is a curiously claustrophobic tragedy of lust and revenge with a characteristically Calvinist sense of immanent damnation hanging over its protagonists.

In criticism Dillon (2007) is a most accessible and enlightening introduction to the notion of tragedy in Shakespeare. McEachern (2003) offers an excellent overview of the development, contexts and nature of Shakespearean tragedy, and of their critical reception and performance history. Smith and Sullivan (2010) is a fine introduction to tragedy beyond Shakespeare, with essays on plays covered in this chapter. More difficult, but certainly accessible, is Belsey (1985), which deals very interestingly with early modern tragedy and gender. Woodbridge (2010) specifically for this period and Kerrigan (1996) more generally offer contrasting views of revenge tragedy. Hopkins (2008) and Coleman (2010) are very good introductions to Marlowe and Webster respectively.

3

NEOCLASSICISM, RESTORATION TRAGEDY AND SENTIMENTALITY

CONTEXTS

France did not develop the kind of secular professional theatre seen in England or Spain in the sixteenth century. By the 1640s, however, the Paris stage had become the most prestigious in Europe. Under Louis XIV France had become the dominant military and political power on the continent, and the King had centralised power into the hands of the monarchy. He also sought cultural supremacy. The theatre which developed under the patronage of the King and the aristocracy successfully appropriated the prestige of classical drama and sought to establish the pre-eminent status of French as a literary language.

The tragedies of Pierre Corneille (1606–84) brought French neoclassical tragedy – a new version of the ancient genre – to full development. This was drama which prided itself upon its rationality and its sense of decorum: an elevated poetic style which it claimed suited the nobility of the characters and ideas presented. The classical unities of time, place and action (see above, p. 15), as reinterpreted by the Italian humanist writer Lodovico Castelvetro's 1570 'Popularisation' of Aristotle's *Poetics* became the inflexible formal structure of both comedy and tragedy, but there was also an 'unwritten, fourth unity: that of tone' (Howarth 1995: 227)

Written entirely in rhyming hexameter lines, the language of French neoclassical tragedy was elegant and musical. Only noble characters appeared on stage. Greek tragedy – not the violence of Seneca – together with subjects from classical history and the bible, formed the subject matter.

Louis XIV's court was the refuge for the exiled English court, following the Royalist defeat in the Civil Wars with Parliament, and when Charles II returned as monarch in 1660 (the 'Restoration') he brought the theatre entirely under royal patronage. The new English tragedies did not entirely mimic the formal rigidity of French drama, but writers still sought to emulate the Parisian model to which the court had been exposed. Even though there was quite often a specific subtext referring to contemporary politics, the personal, rather than the political, lives of monarchs and the nobility became the subject for tragedy.

The theatre's close association with the nobility tainted it with the perceived immorality of Charles's court. This ensured that the stage had its critics, and one of its principal opponents, Thomas Rymer, insisted in 1678 that tragedy must have a didactic moral purpose: 'whoever writes a Tragedy cannot please but must also profit; 'tis the physic [medicine] of the mind that he makes palatable' (Wheatley 2000: 71). Tragic protagonists in these plays often do not fall through their own error of judgement: it is the moral lesson taught to the audience by their fall, and their reaction to their fall, that counted. Rather than challenge its audience to think radically, these plays set out to provide conventional moral instruction. The tragedy of earlier in the century came to be seen as uncouth and morally suspect. Restoration tragedy, at least on the surface, tended to close down the possibilities for thoughtful or socially critical audience reaction in terms of the breadth of their possible response.

The stimulation of the audience's emotions was in fact a principal aim. The dramatist John Dryden answered Rymer by arguing that 'Suffering of Innocence and Punishment of the Offender, is of the Nature of English Tragedy': the production of pity and a sense of justice neatly done (Wheatley 2000: 74). Philosophers such as Descartes (see below, p. 87) thought it was morally and psychologically beneficial for the audience to weep at the unhappy fate of the innocent, especially if it was undeserved.

The focus on the psychology of audience reaction rather than on the play itself can then be regarded as drawing the political sting of the genre in this period (R. Williams 1979: 27). In the eighteenth century the teachings of of the philosopher John Locke took Descartes's ideas further. The capacity to respond sensitively to experiences was seen to be a sign of greater awareness of beauty and morality. Tragedy provided that opportunity. It's significant that another Enlightenment philosopher, David Hume, wrote in 1777 about our emotional response to tragedy rather than the content of the plays themselves in a time when few tragedies of any merit seemed to be produced in Britain.

A significant event on the English stage after 1660 was that women actors began to perform. For the first time also female playwrights had their work produced on the London stage. Aphra Behn was the trailblazer here with her only pure tragedy *Abdelazer* (1676) (Behn 2006).

DESCARTES ON THE PASSIONS

Attitudes towards the expression of the emotions changed during the seventeenth century. In the Renaissance the classical belief that the emotions were a kind of psychological disturbance which had to be kept under control had some influence. Aristotle had apparently taught that tragedy could purge harmful emotions (see above, p. 16) and the Stoics thought that powerful feelings could hinder the rational pursuit of virtue (see above, p. 39). But, as the study of nature according to scientific principles gained currency, the idea that the passions (as they were called), were a healthy and normal part of human nature became established. The French philosopher René Descartes (1596–1650) published *The Passions of the Soul* in 1649. He argued that the passions 'are useful because they strengthen and prolong thoughts that it is good for the soul to have and which otherwise might easily be wiped out' (Descartes 2015: 21). With regard to pity, people who genuinely feel compassion are the 'most generous' and 'most strong-minded' in their ability to resist fear for the future. The sadness 'caused by tragic actions represented on the stage' gives the soul a sense of satisfaction that it is doing its natural duty (52). He concludes that 'persons whom the passions can move most deeply are capable of enjoying the sweetest pleasures of this life' (58). Under the influence of this kind of thinking tragedy in this period became an opportunity for audiences to emote healthily, but also to show a moral superiority in their public display of feeling which would justify their social superiority at a time when audiences of London and Paris were becoming less socially mixed. Tragedy became sentimental.

JEAN RACINE, *PHAEDRA* (1677)

The French dramatist Jean Racine (1639–99) wrote a series of tragedies remarkable for their taut intensity and condensed power. In this play Racine drew more on Euripides' version of the story of Phaedra and Hippolytus than Seneca's (see above, p. 39). Hippolytus, the illegitimate son of Theseus, King of Athens, is determined to leave Trezene, where the court is in residence during the King's prolonged absence. His stepmother, Phaedra, is wasting away through her undeclared incestuous passion for Hippolytus. When word comes of Theseus's apparent death she cannot help telling him how she feels. Disgusted, Hippolytus draws his sword, which she grabs from him as she flees, startled at the arrival of Hippolytus's friend Theramenes. Almost immediately word comes that Theseus is in fact alive and will soon be with them. Phaedra is persuaded by her old nurse Oenone to claim that Hippolytus tried to rape her – she has his sword for proof. Hippolytus's sense of honour will not let him tell the truth and accuse Theseus's wife, and he is exiled by his father with a curse on his head. Hippolytus arranges to meet his lover, Aricia, outside the city so they can flee to Athens, but Poseidon, god of the sea, answers Theseus's curse and sends a sea monster to attack him. As Theramenes reports in the conventional messenger speech at the play's climax, Hippolytus wounds the monster but his chariot horses bolt. Entangled in the reins, he is dragged to his death.

Aricia finds his mutilated body. Phaedra admits the truth to her husband, then dies from the poison she has taken.

All Racine's plays were written in rhyming hexameter lines, employing a remarkably restrained range of vocabulary and, often, a pristine simplicity of expression. There's a sense of elegant constraint in the form of the work. The mishaps of the tragedy follow in rapid succession to a small group of characters who seem locked into an inescapable chain of events. Hippolytus famously begins the play by declaring that 'it's all determined' that he will leave Trezene (Racine 2013a: 209, 1.1.1), but we know that the fate of all the characters in neoclassical tragedy will be restricted to this single location. Dominating the whole play is the figure of Phaedra, a character whose speeches achieve a passionate and dramatic intensity which makes the other characters seem two-dimensional in their representation. As Simon Critchley writes, 'Oenone is little more than a sounding board for Phaedra's essentially solitary dialogues, Theseus is something of a flatfooted oaf throughout, and poor, virginal Hippolytus is an unworthy object of such ferocious desire' (Critchley 2008: 189).

Racine was educated in a college, Port-Royal, which taught a distinctive branch of French Catholicism, Jansenism, a doctrine which in some ways seems more like Calvinism (see above, p. 46). For Jansenists, the world was an irremediably fallen and wicked place from which its Creator had totally withdrawn Himself. The only valid action for the Christian is to retreat into solitude away from life in the world. The French scholar Lucien Goldman argued that Jansenism was the key to understanding Racine's tragedies. There exists an unseen figure in these plays outside time 'who demands the realization of an absolute justice alien to any compromise', who 'makes life impossible' and 'whose sentence disregards any motive or explanation … and who judges nothing but the *act*' (Goldman 1972: 9, 10). Phaedra, according to Goldman, is a heroic figure, with a 'full presence' who 'lives in search of reality', with an 'unremitting need for happiness and purity' which drives her passion for the weak, naïve Hippolytus (90, 91). But this is a dream. Hippolytus represents the fallen, compromised world; 'she loves him with a purity which, were it really to exist, would make him inaccessible' (91). She cannot but strive for a perfection which this world cannot provide, only to be condemned by an inexorable, inaccessible force which condemns her for seeking the perfection which demonstrates the reality of that very force. Such purity exists elsewhere but is impossible in a sinful world. Contrary to 'the traditional interpretation', Goldman writes, 'it is Hippolytus's unreality and weakness and Phaedra's full and real presence which characterise and constitute the universe of Racine's tragedy' (91).

This is a very stark view of existence, but the power of Racine's play renders it plausible in its own terms. An even starker account of the tragic vision of *Phaedra* has been developed by Simon Critchley. Phaedra is the daughter of King Minos, once of Crete but who now sits in judgement of the dead in the underworld. She knows that there is no escape from shame and torture for her even in death (250, 4.6.1276–88). For Critchley this speaks eloquently of the tragic condition of human identity he finds in the work of the philosopher Emmanuel Levinas, where our sense of who we are is always trying impossibly to escape the randomness of the historical facts that create who we are, a 'burden of facticity that weighs one down without one's ever being able to pick it up' (Critchley 2008: 170). Phaedra is the creature of her own heredity, the daughter of a lustful mother, Pasiphaë, who had sex with a monster, the Minotaur, and the granddaughter of the Sun, which represents absolute moral judgement – God. Her fate is already running ahead of her 'and this is why she is so utterly fatigued' (Critchley 2008: 186). But Phaedra cannot die and escape pain in this play. For Critchley the 'corpse on stage at the end of the play' is the world we live in: 'the moral of the tragedy is that life in the world is impossible.' The political world of the play is rendered 'a farce of force … it is senseless.' Without God he thinks there is no tragedy here, for in that case the play 'is reduced to being some story about a crazy woman trying to commit incest at court' (Critchley 2008: 179, 191, 193). Despite, or perhaps because of the tight formal constraints of neoclassicism and Christian dogma, Racine's *Phaedra* retains the power to provoke questions about the need for some kind of absolute force, whether divine, metaphysical, moral or political to give meaning to our sense of the tragic.

JOHN DRYDEN, *ALL FOR LOVE* (1677)

This exact English contemporary of Racine's play is a much less intense piece of work. This version of the story of Antony and Cleopatra claimed to have gone back to the ancient sources in order to find the most 'favourable' portrait of its Roman protagonist, and not just rework Shakespeare (Dryden 1986: 10). Dryden's play begins with Antony in Egypt after Actium (see above, p. 75). Depressed by defeat, Antony is persuaded by his general Ventidius to abandon Cleopatra and resume the fight against his rival for control of the empire, Octavius Caesar. But when (against Venditius's advice) Antony agrees to bid her farewell one last time he cannot resist returning to her side again. In Act Three Ventidius, assisted now by Antony's friend Dolabella once more attempts to part him from the Egyptian Queen. They bring in Antony's wife, Caesar's sister Octavia, with their children, and Antony once more renounces Cleopatra, who then engages in an undignified row with Octavia. In Act Four Ventidius sets up Dolabella to flirt with Cleopatra in order finally to prove to Antony her untrustworthiness. Cleopatra has also been advised by her Eunuch Alexas to make Antony jealous by the same means to try to win him back. Neither Dolabella nor Cleopatra can keep up the pretence with each other but when Antony is told of their apparent betrayal he furiously denounces both. Octavia abandons him. Alexas tells Antony that Cleopatra is dead. He hopes that this will make Antony acknowledge his true feelings for Cleopatra and that his mistress will reward her eunuch for this service. Antony does take this as proof of her love but resolves on suicide himself since, as he says, his life is now meaningless. Ventidius kills himself rather than Antony as ordered. Antony stabs himself and dies in Cleopatra's arms. She commits suicide by applying a poisonous snake to herself as she sits on her throne dressed in all her regalia next to Antony's corpse: 'the chief persons represented were famous patterns of unlawful love, and their end accordingly was unfortunate' (10).

The twentieth-century critic F. R. Leavis wrote that, when considering *All for Love*, Shakespeare's *Antony and Cleopatra* 'has an actuality, a richness and a depth in comparison with which it becomes absurd to discuss Dryden's play as a tragedy' (Leavis

1968: 106). This may be taking things too far, but there is certainly something artificial and limited about the play. 'A chamber, neoclassical distillation of the famous story' is how David Roberts (2014: 105) charitably puts it (by 'chamber' he means that the action has a domestic setting, with a relatively small cast, in contrast to Shakespeare's epic depiction of the story; see above, p. 74). Each act is a dramatic set-piece in its own right on the question, 'Will he leave her?' But rather than being merely repetitious, this playing on the same note again and again foregrounds the play's central contrast, between Cleopatra's unflinching constancy and Antony's vacillating infidelity. In insisting on the irrational but unarguable ultimate supremacy of the protagonists' love over every other consideration, Dryden is insisting on the power of an absolute force against which human life must founder: not God, as in Racine, but loyalty. In the era of absolute monarchy, tragedy shows the justice but also the pathos of this foundering. It is I think a narrow and authoritarian view of tragedy.

The play might be seen to portray women, the traditional trope of inconstancy, in a very poor light. The duologue between Cleopatra and Octavia at the end of Act Three depicts them both as vain and shallow, with Cleopatra sneering at Octavia's lack of physical 'charms' and thanking 'bounteous Nature' and 'indulgent Heaven' for her own attributes 'to please the bravest man' (72; 3.444–7). To the Romans she is promiscuous and treacherous. Octavia tells her that Antony is 'not the first/ For whom you spread your snares'; she is no more than a 'faithless prostitute' (71; 3.428–9: 88; 4.389). Ventidius tells Alexas to confirm 'each nightly change [of lovers] she makes'. She is 'every man's Cleopatra' (86; 4.324: 85; 4.299). But as J. Douglas Canfield has pointed out, Dryden in fact goes out of his way to stress Cleopatra's fidelity, to the point of showing that Antony was her first love, and that she was subsequently forced into a relationship with Julius Caesar against her will ('He first possess'd my person; you my love,' she tells Antony). At Actium she fled out of fear, and did not change sides. She turns down Octavius's offers to retain her kingdom if she will hand over Antony (52; 2.354: 53; 2.375–6, 390–405; Canfield 1989: 238–39). She is figured by, and associated with jewels throughout the play (46; 2.199–200: 80; 4.204–6: 107; 5.365–69: 109; 5.437; Canfield 1989: 242–43).

By contrast 'after Philippi, Antony left [his wife] Fulvia for Cleopatra only to desert her again and marry Octavia, only to desert her and return to Cleopatra, whom twice within Dryden's play he is prepared to desert again' (Canfield 1989: 241).

Dryden goes against the current of the traditional misogynist portrayal of the faithless Eastern queen to show a kind of hidden constancy beyond reason; it is 'such transcendent passion' that it makes Cleopatra 'soar quite out of reason's view' so that she becomes lost above it; love that makes the rule of the world by comparison a mere child's rattle (40; 20–22: 55; 2.444). Absolute loyalty beyond political advantage is the ultimate value, even if the subject of that loyalty does not seem to merit it. That is what constitutes Cleopatra's tragedy. Restoration plays are often read against the politics of their time. Charles II was known for his mistresses, his favourites and his expediency, but he was the king, and, for 'Tory' loyalists like Dryden, God's anointed monarch; his brother, the future James II to whom absolute loyalty was also owed, was a Catholic. Loyalty in a fallen world to a metaphysical absolute which neither reason nor advantage can shake is a sign of nobility and virtue, but is likely to confer tragic status in neo-classical drama. Tragic pathos here both elevates the mystical nature of royal absolutism and shows its unviability as a concept in the world of real politics. It's historically doomed. As Octavia tells Antony, 'My Lord, my Lord, love will not always last' (88; 4.416).

THOMAS OTWAY, *VENICE PRESERV'D* (1682)

Of all the tragedies written in this period Otway's *Venice Preserv'd* had the longest afterlife on the London stage and was performed well into the nineteenth century. Its main roles were regarded as opportunities for virtuoso acting and by reputation it was thought nearly the equal of Shakespeare's tragedies (Kelsall 1969: xvii).

Otway's source was an account of a Spanish-backed attempted coup against the Venetian state in 1618. The protagonist, Jaffeir, joins the conspiracy at the instigation of his friend, the soldier Pierre. Pierre's hatred of the corrupt oligarchy which runs the city is motivated by the fact that his lover, the courtesan Aquilina, is the mistress of Antonio, a senator. Jaffeir is married to Belvidera, the daughter of another senator, Priuli, against the father's wishes.

Priuli has caused Jaffeir's creditors to foreclose on his debts and at the beginning of the play he is destitute. The conspirators, who think they have corrupted Venice's mercenary army, plan to assassinate the Senate and seize power amidst arson and general bloodshed. They are suspicious of Jaffeir as a latecomer to their plot. He offers his wife Belvidera as a hostage, giving the chief conspirator, Renault, a dagger to stab her if he should betray their cause. But Renault tries to rape Belvidera, and she persuades her husband that they should inform the Senate of their danger. In anguish Jaffeir agrees, and obtains a promise from the authorities to pardon the lives of the twenty-two conspirators. But his information comes too late, for the conspirators have just been detected. The Senate go back on their promise, and Pierre strikes Jaffeir and accuses him of betrayal. The increasingly manic Jaffeir tries ineffectually to fulfil his promise and stab Belvidera. She persuades her father to beg the Senate to pardon the offenders, but in vain. Jaffeir joins Pierre on the scaffold and they are reconciled. Jaffeir kills his friend that he may die a noble death, rather than at the hands of the public executioner, then stabs himself. Belvidera goes mad and dies, scratching at the ground as the ghosts of Jaffeir and Pierre rise before her.

The corruption of the Venetian ruling class is made clear in the comic scenes where Antonio begs his mistress Aquilina to spit on him and kick him while he pretends to be a dog. But this only echoes the masochistic Jaffeir in his relationships with both Belvidera and Pierre. The conspirators are a brutal and murderous bunch, intending to replace one aristocratic tyranny with another, to

> lop their nobles
> To the base roots, whence most of 'em first sprung;
> Enslave the rout, whom smarting will make humble;
> Turn out their droning Senate, and possess
> That seat of empire which our souls were framed for.
>
> (Otway 1969: 30–31; 2.3.79–82)

The immediate context of the play was the so-called 'Popish Plot' of 1678, a hysterically rumoured Catholic uprising. Strangely, the play became a lightning conductor for political radicals in the 1790s

(McEvoy 2016:43–46) despite its failure to depict any admirable personal or political qualities. Critics have pointed to the play's depiction of a society where human identity fluctuates ('irregular man's ne'er constant, never certain', as Renault says; 28; 2.3.12), where people think neither logically nor abstractly but in an 'uncontrolled sequence of discrete sensory images' (Hughes 1996:301), and often graphically sexualised ones at that. The language of the three main characters is full of passionate and desperate exclamations. By the end of the play honesty, faithfulness, trust, virtue have all been replaced by 'meaningless gestures, mad ravings and nonsense' (Canfield 2000: 101), such as that spouted by the senator Antonio (82; 5.2.1–26). The conspirators claim nobility but glory in their cruel violence, and indeed seem to get a sexual kick out of it, as does Jaffeir (53; 3.2.321; 54; 373–88; 46 14–49; Canfield 2000: 104–5). The senate are perjured and callous. 'Denied absolutes', writes Derek Hughes 'humanity is left … only with the conflicting impulses of the body, which toss man between servility and impotent dreams of freedom' (Hughes 1996: 306).

Venice Preserv'd is a remarkable play in that it exposes the shaky ground on which English Restoration tragedy is based, and also looks forward to a much later notion of tragedy when life seems meaningless and desperate. In setting the play in a republic where the rulers were at least nominally elected by their peers the Tory Otway might be seen to be showing the depths of universal moral degradation to which a state without a monarch (as England had been only twenty-three years before) can sink. Jaffeir, Belvidera and Pierre are supposed to be noble, tragic figures in a world where truth and honesty have vanished but have become creatures of sadistic, masochistic, fetishistic desires. In a world where the absolute monarch is supposed to be the divinely sanctioned answer to all injustice tragedy in fact ought to be impossible, since obedience to his will and trust in power resolves all questions. In the contemporary French comedy *Tartuffe* (1667), for example, it emerges that the King has known all the wickedness that has been going on and his messenger arrives to produce a happy ending when all seemed lost (Molière 2002: 84). If the absolute source of justice is implausible in Dryden's *All for Love* (see above, p. 91), in *Venice Preserv'd* the consequences of its absence might be seen as a validation of its necessity, but in fact the tragic power of the play lies in the psychological credibility of the nightmarish actions of its protagonists, the feature which has made the play popular with actors and audiences (Kelsall 1969: xix–xxii). In a culture built on an ideological fiction, Otway, probably unintentionally, shows the violent nihilism that underlies the aristocratic right to rule and its codes of justice and loyalty, leaving a frighteningly modern vision of human degradation. This is not a play that provides 'physic of the mind' (see above, p. 86) but achieves a genuine tragic pathos in performance because it cannot do so.

DAVID HUME, *ON TRAGEDY* (1757)

In 1757 the Scottish philosopher and historian David Hume set out to explain why we experience pleasure when we watch suffering in a tragedy, encountering scenes which in real life would cause us such distress. Yet we choose to watch such things on stage and get enjoyment from it. Hume's answer was that there are two feelings which are aroused in tragedy. The first is indeed the pain caused by the apprehension of the suffering, but the second, predominant one, is the pleasure we get from the skill of the playwright and the actor: 'the force of imagination, the energy of expression, the power of numbers [the metrical effects of poetry upon us, but also perhaps of rhetorical figures], the charms of imitation; all these are naturally, of themselves delightful to the mind' (Hume 1993: 131). In such cases the predominant feeling overpowers the weaker one, and takes greater force from the subordinate emotion, increasing the pleasure further: 'the whole impulse of those passions is converted into pleasure, and swells the delight, which the eloquence raises in us' (129). In addition tragedy, like painting, is an imitation of reality, and imitation always provides us with pleasure.

When the nastiness of what is depicted on stage reaches a certain point, however, no artistic skill can produce enough pleasure to overwhelm our distaste, and then the audience is disgusted ('the English theatre abounds too much with such shocking images', he writes primly; 132). To depict the virtuous suffering 'under the triumphant tyranny and oppression of vice' requires the playwright to show 'noble courageous despair, or the vice receive its proper punishment' otherwise 'disagreeable spectacle' is the outcome (132–3). Hume's theory of tragedy is too narrow to convince. The fate of Belvidera in *Venice Preserv'd* does not fit this criterion and drew audiences in his day again and again to the theatre. Neither will it fit so much early modern or contemporary tragedy. But the idea that the elegant shaping of a piece of drama can represent 'the forces of rightness and beneficence' and provide an emotional counterweight to the horrors of tragedy was revived in the twentieth century (Kitto 1966:142).

FURTHER READING

Nahum Tate's version of Shakespeare's *King Lear* is the most notorious example of how neoclassical tragedy attempted to tame the raw power of its predecessors (Tate 1997). Corneille's great *Cinna* (Corneille 2013) and Racine's intense *Andromache* (Racine 2013b) are other important French neoclassical works. James and Jondorf (1994) offer a detailed contextualisation and commentary on Racine's *Phaedra*. Wallace (2007) draws some interesting parallels between the tragic visions of Seneca and Racine. Wheatley (2000) provides a good introduction to Restoration Tragedy and Hughes (1996) a fuller survey of the development of the genre. Canfield (2000) shows how the politics and ideology of the period informed that development.

4

'FROM HERO TO VICTIM'

ROMANTIC TRAGEDY AND AFTER

CONTEXTS

The huge advances made in science and technology in Europe in the late-seventeenth and eighteenth centuries seemed to demonstrate the triumph of reason and to suggest that human beings had the capacity to transform the conditions under which they lived permanently for the better. But they also produced a reaction against rationalism itself, and a desire to assert the primacy of emotion in human identity and the idea that humans are part of nature, not its dominators.

The changes in European thought and culture which became known as **Romanticism** were already underway when Britain's American colonies declared themselves in 1776 an independent republic dedicated to 'life, liberty and the pursuit of happiness'. In politics romanticism was often democratic in sentiment and an enemy of the arbitrary rule of hereditary monarchs. As the Swiss philosopher Jean-Jacques Rousseau began his 1762 book *The Social Contract*, 'man was born free and everywhere he is in chains' (Rousseau 2008: 45). When the French revolutionaries executed their monarch in 1793 and proclaimed a republic based on 'liberty, equality and fraternity' the more idealistic of them sought to refound a whole society on rational and 'natural' principles.

Despite the descent of revolutionary idealism into mass purges and factional murder in the 'Terror', and the suborning of the revolution into military dictatorship by Napoleon Bonaparte, the ideals of the revolution remained popular throughout Europe, especially when governments tried to restore the old hierarchies and restrictions on free expression in the years after Napoleon's defeat in 1815. Despite being a self-styled emperor Napoleon remained for Romantics an image of the man of low birth who made the world in his own image by the force of his will.

In the theatre Romantic writers sought to express this new vision and shake off the weight of past tradition. It has been claimed that they failed; even that tragedy was impossible for them to write. In a democratic age when one man's intrinsic worth was regarded as no greater than any others, there was no room for a tragic hero with 'greatness of soul' (see above, p. 17). George Steiner (see below, p. 127) wrote that if a culture believes in human perfectibility, then suffering is not the product of some fall from grace, nor of some flaw in human nature, nor of the operation of some 'inexplicable and destructive forces' (Steiner 1961: 128). Rather, for the Romantics, it arose 'from the absurdities and archaic inequalities built into the social fabric by generations of tyrants and exploiters. The chains of man, proclaimed Rousseau, were man-forged. They could be broken by human hammers' (Steiner 1961: 125). Tragedy in such a culture is impossible: 'the destiny of [Shakespeare's] Lear', he quips, 'cannot be resolved by the establishment of adequate homes for the aged' (Steiner 1961: 128).

But this is to assume that the Romantics achieved the world they desired and perfected humanity. In fact Romantic literature is full of its own sense of the limits and even failure of Romantic aspiration in the real world, while nevertheless 'trying to discover heroism in modern man's attempt to live in a world cut off from the God of tradition and denied a vision of an ideal future' (Cox 1987: xiii). While striving to make a new world in the imagination – a faculty most precious to them – they also became aware of what had been lost in the ordered society of the past, of the alienation and self-consciousness brought by the new sense of individualism, and often of the violent destruction which was central to the revolutions which sought to free people from various oppressions. 'What happens,' wrote Jeffrey N. Cox, when 'man finds that he has destroyed the closed world of the traditional order, but that he is unable to break through to the open world of the romantic imagination?' (Cox 1987: 3) (or indeed women, who become an important part of the literary, if not dramatic, scene in this period). In this sense of failure, tragedy was inherent in the Romantic project.

In Britain, where the theatre seemed unable to shake off the influence of Shakespeare and his contemporaries, little serious drama of any originality or merit seems to have emerged in this period, but in Germany in particular important tragic drama was written, if not necessarily valued, in the first decades of the nineteenth century. In France, a new romantic tragedy was deployed in a deliberate assault on **neoclassicism** (see above, p. 85) by Victor Hugo.

A significant reason why tragedy did not prosper in the mid-nineteenth century lies in the increasing domination of the theatre by the growing middle classes, in England in particular, but also elsewhere in Europe and in the United States. The importance of 'respectability' in moral behaviour (especially sexual behaviour) amongst the bourgeoisie also applied to the content of plays, and endings which didn't challenge the notions of **Providence** or of 'poetic justice' became hard to sustain. Romantic passion subsided into melodrama, as can be seen in Hugo's tragedies. But individualism was also a prime virtue of the middle classes. This was an age of *laissez-faire* economics, where the individual pursuit of wealth and advantage was assumed to work for the overall benefit of society. The contradiction evident between a restrictive moral code and the validation of personal self-interest emerged powerfully in the work of the Norwegian playwright Henrik Ibsen (1828–1906) whose plays revivified European tragedy. Taking the form of the middle-class domestic melodrama, Ibsen's late plays such as *Ghosts* (1881) challenged the moral codes those plays had embodied and showed that tragedy could now be reconfigured as the depiction of forces beyond the conscious actions of individual protagonists in a world without divine providence or a beneficent human destiny. The modern tragic protagonist would be a victim, not a hero.

HEINRICH VON KLEIST, *THE PRINCE OF HOMBURG* (1811)

The drama produced in early nineteenth-century Germany perhaps best expresses the energy and anxiety of the period, and also prefigures what tragedy would become in the future. Heinrich von Kleist (1777–1811) had been an officer in the Prussian army and wrote this play just before his death in a suicide pact.

The play is based on a true incident in the seventeenth-century wars between Prussia and Sweden. Prince Friedrich is a cavalry commander who disobeys orders when he leads a successful charge which puts victory at risk at a crucial moment in a battle. Despite the Prussians winning victory he is court-martialled and sentenced to death. At the briefing before the battle, however, the Prince had been distracted by the presence of Princess Natalie, who could not find her glove. In the play's first scene he had been found by the Prussian King ('The Elector') and courtiers weaving a victory wreath in his sleep. The Elector teases the Prince by taking the wreath from him and making the sleepwalking prince try to get it back from Natalie. He only succeeds in snatching her glove from her. When the Prince awakes he can remember nothing but is puzzled by the glove he still holds. After his arrest he believes his pardon is certain, but when he sees his grave being dug he panics and begs for mercy. Natalie intercedes with the Elector, but the monarch will only absolve the Prince if the Prince can himself prove that the sentence was unjust. The Prince cannot, and now welcomes his death, claiming that he wants to see 'the sacred rules of war,/ Which I infringed in full view of the ranks/ Glorified by my voluntary death' (Kleist 2002: 101). Despite petitions and pleas by the army and its officers, the Prince is led out blindfold to face a firing squad on the same castle ramp where he was found asleep in the first scene. But the Elector and Natalie present the wreath to him again, and his pardon seems to be proclaimed to the sound of cannon fire. 'Is this a dream?' he asks. 'A dream? Of course,' replies a senior officer (107).

Although far from classical in form, Kleist's play has many of the authentic qualities of classical tragedy which Lessing had identified as more important to the nature of tragedy than the formal rules beloved of the neoclassicists (see below, p. 85). Like

Sophocles' *Antigone* (see above, p. 21) it deals with a noble character fatally involved in a clash between principles, in this case the impartiality of the military code and human mercy (or alternatively what Sean Allan calls 'the common sense world … and a make-believe world of heroic bravura and unworkable "iron" discipline'; Allan 1996: 225). The scope of the action, from battlefield to prison to palace, and the tone, which is comic in places, show Kleist's own immersion in Shakespearean tragedy. Yet the play appears to have a happy ending (as did some of Euripides' last tragedies such as *Helen*; see above, p. 18). The playwright Dennis Kelly, clearly dissatisfied, produced a version more conventionally tragic in London in 2010, which ended in the Prince's execution but with the refusal of the court and army to join in the Elector's acclamation that the Prince's last wish had been fulfilled (Kleist 2010: 90). In the original we suspect that we may be watching a dream and the Prince's fate remains uncertain. There remains a feeling that we have been watching a tragedy.

The Prince certainly constructs himself as a conventional tragic protagonist in his claim that he is dying selflessly so that his nation can learn from his error of judgement to its own greater glory, and he speaks a final heroic monologue where he can feel himself being transformed into an immortal spirit (105). Yet there is something flimsy and unconvincing about this.

In the opening scene the Prince's weaving of his hero's wreath only happens in a dream. Real life is full of confusion and error. At the military briefing and on the battlefield the Elector is thought dead then found to be alive. The Prince's feelings are confused and unpredictable. His nervous collapse (which led to the play's first production in 1821 being closed down on the grounds that it was detrimental to military morale; Allan 1996: 224) is just one symptom of his inability to find secure grounds for what he really thinks or how he should act, as is his confusion about whether the girl in his dream was just the real Natalie or some heavenly figure (27). Neither can he decide whether the Elector is a father-figure to him or a tyrant who will sacrifice him to clear the way to marry off Natalie for political expedience. Only by renouncing his humanity and embracing the inhuman coldness of the Elector's decree can he free himself from the torment of Romantic self-consciousness. But that heroic death turns into a dream.

The Elector, on the other hand, tries to control the confusion of a world where there is no divine **Providence** nor benevolent direction to history by imposing an absolute impartial law. But when he sees the consequence of this, the destruction of a man whom he admires in opposition to the will of the court and army, he tries to turn this absolute law into a contract by making the Prince agree with his sentence (Cox 1987: 242). He sees the law to be just a human construct, and turns his act of mercy into a staged triumph of the Prussian state. The action and plot of the play are heroic, but the world of the play is relativistic and uncertain. *The Prince of Homburg* points to a major shift of the notion and meaning of the tragic:

> The tragic ceases to describe the fate of the individual hero; it becomes the central fact of human existence. The world, tragically, lacks a final meaningful order; and the order that modern culture must create to shape this chaos has no room for tragedy, no room for heroes. Kleist's tragic vision arises from his sense that life is neither a dream from which we awake to discover the divine, nor a stage with heroic actors struggling to break through into vision; life is chaos, and the dream and the theatre are man's only defences against it.
>
> (Cox 1987: 250)

A new kind of tragic theatre was emerging.

THE ASSAULT ON NEOCLASSICISM: GOTTHOLD LESSING AND VICTOR HUGO

The German dramatist and literary theorist Gotthold Lessing (1729–81) was one of the first to offer a convincing demolition of neoclassical tragedy in his *Hamburg Dramaturgy* (1767–8). He argued that neoclassicism was not the true inheritor of the Greek tradition. In fact it was not classical at all. In emphasising the significance of formal conventions such as the unities (see above, p. 15), they had missed the most significant continuity between Sophocles and Shakespeare, which existed in structures of belief and feeling: in the sincerity in religious and supernatural belief found in both, in the depth of genuine pity and fear (see above, p. 16) elicited in the audience, and in the coherence and believability of the characterisation and plotting. Neoclassical tragedy used the supernatural as a hollow artifice; furthermore its 'stately heroes ... solicit from us cold admiration. These characters would bridle at our pity'. The plotting can too often depend on 'incredible dramatic coincidences and foreshortening ... what Aristotle meant by unity was inner coherence and poetic logic as it is exhibited in *Othello* or *Macbeth*' (Steiner 1961: 190). This is not necessarily true. As Raymond Williams pointed out, Lessing was articulating 'a mid-eighteenth century version of Greek tragedy and Shakespeare in which the true common factor is the mid-eighteenth century' (Williams 1979: 28–9). Yet Lessing licensed the later Romantic veneration of Shakespeare and permanently undermined neoclassicism.

Even so, in the early nineteenth century neoclassicism was still overwhelmingly dominant in French theatre (despite the increasing popularity of the recently arrived Shakespeare on the Paris stage) when the young poet and playwright Victor Hugo (1802–85) wrote his Preface to his play *Cromwell* (1827). In this Preface Hugo sets out a manifesto for the Romantic drama which he felt must replace neoclassicism in the theatre. Hugo asserts that the Christian age requires a different literature from the classical. Whereas the classical view of humanity sees only a lofty nobility, Christianity acknowledges that human beings are composed of both the physical body and the spiritual soul, and that it is both natural and truthful for both to be shown on the stage, for:

> the one is perishable, the other immortal; the one is physical, the other is ethereal; the one is enchained by its appetites, needs and passions, the other is carried away on the wings of enthusiasm and dreams ... the style of the drama is then realism; realism is the result of the natural combination of

two qualities, the sublime and the grotesque, which meet each other in the drama, just as they meet each other in life and in all creation.

(cited in Howarth 1975: 130, my translation)

The master of this style of theatre who must be emulated is Shakespeare. Hugo's Romantic tragedy *Hernani* was provocatively produced in Paris in 1830 cheered on by a claque of avant-garde artists, and the result was rioting in the playhouse (McEvoy 2016: 67ff.). But Hugo's reformulation led not to a rebirth of tragedy as realism; rather, with its advocacy of sentiment and sensation, it contributed to the dominance of **melodrama** in the nineteenth century.

GEORG BÜCHNER, *WOYZECK* (1836)

Like Kleist, Büchner lived a brief life, dying from typhus in 1837 at the age of 23. Büchner held radical egalitarian political views for which he was persecuted. He published an impassioned tragedy about the politics of the French Revolution, in censored form, *Danton's Death*, in 1835.

Woyzeck was unfinished at the time of his death. The drafts were rediscovered many years later and the play was published in a reconstructed form in 1877. Its first performance was in Munich in 1913. It's an important play in the history of the development of tragedy not just because it represents the full expression of the complexity of romantic ideas in the genre, but also because it points so clearly to the tragedies of the future. Büchner did not set out to make any kind of moral point. 'The highest task' of the playwright, he wrote in 1835, 'is to come as close as possible to the historical event as it really happened. His work should not be any more nor any less moral than history itself' (cited in Schwartz 1978: 43).

All of the tragedies in this book so far were written in verse (with the exception of parts of those by Shakespeare and Webster). *Woyzeck* is written entirely in prose, as will be all the plays discussed from now on. The play's protagonist is not a nobleman, but is based on a real-life mercenary soldier who murdered his wife in 1821. The case became a sensation, and, after academic debate about whether he was sane enough to be accountable for his actions, Johann Woyzeck was beheaded in Leipzig in 1824. Büchner's Woyzeck is a troubled and disturbed soldier who kills his lover Marie because she has been unfaithful to him with a Drum-Major. The play consists of episodes and feels fragmentary. Woyzeck and Marie watch performing animals at a fair; Woyzeck shaves his Captain, who is full of strange fears and melancholies; Woyzeck is reprimanded by a doctor for urinating in the street (he is paid by this doctor to be a specimen for examination, it seems); he hears a drunken apprentice preach on God's purpose for creating mankind while he is enraged at seeing Marie dancing with the Drum-Major.

The play's protagonist is an ordinary man and his crime apparently sordid but the play asks as profound questions as had previous tragedies which were concerned with the fate of princes. The play in its most finished form is keen to stress the common humanity of rich and poor. Marie asserts that she has 'just as red a mouth as the great ladies with their mirrors from top to toe' (Büchner 2012: 140), even if, as John Reddick writes, this 'essential humanness ... is already in the process of securing Marie's own doom' (Reddick 1994: 306). But *Woyzeck* is not merely a trite, if valid, political assertion or a sigh at some notion of the fallen nature of human sexuality. In its events and in its language the play presents its characters as significantly similar to animals: the performing monkeys and the horse at the fairground which have been taught to behave like humans 'through the effect of art'; the horse that can count 'behaves improperly', presumably in the same manner as Woyzeck did according to the doctor. According to the Carnival Announcer, 'a beastly human being' is 'still an animal' (139–40). The characters' language is full of reference to animals, and they constantly address one another as animals. The Jew from whom Woyzeck buys the murder weapon calls him a 'dog' and when Woyzeck rages at the thought of Marie's infidelity ('everything can roll around in lust, man and woman, man and beast') he compares them to flies copulating on his hand (149, 147). But if Woyzeck and Marie and the Drum-

Major are creatures of animal impulse which human culture has precariously and perhaps deludedly transformed from 'dust, sand and dirt', can we hold them responsible for their actions? Buchner's play examines 'questions of civilization as against nature; moral choice against animal compulsion; responsibility and accountability; crime and punishment; sin and retribution' (Reddick 1994: 308).

The play's own language is full of a frustrated failure of expression, yet is of great power despite its broken, jagged, elliptical quality. George Steiner wrote that 'Woyzeck's agonised spirit hammers in vain on the doors of language. The fluency of his tormentors, the doctor and the Captain, is the more horrible because what they say should not be dignified with literate speech' (Steiner 1961: 275). 'The words at his command', he writes, 'are inadequate to the pressure and savagery of his feeling. The result is a kind of terrifying simplicity' (Steiner 1961: 280):

> Are you freezing Marie? But you're warm. How hot your lips are! – Hot, the hot breath of a whore – and yet I'd give heaven and earth to kiss them once more. And when you're cold, you don't freeze anymore. The morning dew won't make you freeze.
>
> (152)

Jennifer Wallace writes that 'tragedies perform the moments of suffering's successful or unsuccessful translation into language with problematic consequences. In drama, we see the ambiguous transmutation in *process*, not its successful *results*' (Wallace 2007: 113). If Kleist's *Prince of Homburg* showed a whole society and culture crafted as a fiction against chaos, Büchner's *Woyzeck* shows individual humans struggle (and fail) to assert their rational, moral natures against the animality of their 'natures'. Yet the crafted language and dramatic art which seeks to articulate this assault on human dignity and self-worth suggests that there exists a transcendent quality to our efforts which lacks the substance of the old absolute qualities – whether sanctioned by God or the idea of immutable human hierarchies – but is still there. The insubstantiality of this quality which seeks fully to express the nature of suffering can be seen a tragic fact, and perhaps comprises the nature of tragedy as an art form itself. After the German

Romantics, tragedy would often take on a different meaning informed by humanism in its modern sense, rather than by religion; 'a shaping spirit of aspiration and dignity and compassion' (R. Williams 1979: 29).

HENRIK IBSEN, *HEDDA GABLER* (1890)

Ibsen's dramas often take the form of a domestic **melodrama** yet also challenge the conventional moral pieties of their age: the contrast between form and content serves to make their dramatic impact all the more potent.

Hedda, the daughter of a Norwegian army general whose portrait hangs prominently on the stage, has just returned from her honeymoon with her husband, the cultural history lecturer Jörgen Tesman. It becomes clear that she did not marry out of love and that she feels frustrated and constrained in her new life. She is irritated by the attentions of her husband's aunt and bored by what she sees as the triviality of Jörgen's research into medieval crafts. She seems sexually frustrated too, and appears to accept the attentions of Mr Brack, a judge who is a friend of her husband. An old schoolfellow of Hedda's, Thea Elvsted, suddenly arrives. She announces that she has left her husband and has become the lover of an academic rival of Jörgen, Ejlert Lövborg, a fiery character with a drink problem. It emerges that Lövborg had also been involved with Hedda, and that she had defended her honour by threatening him with one of her father's pistols, the same weapon she uses to take a playful potshot at Brack. Jörgen and Lövborg get very drunk at a party at Brack's house. Lövborg drops the manuscript of a new book which Jörgen finds and gives to Hedda for safe keeping. She later burns it having not revealed to Lövborg that she is in possession of this 'child' (Ibsen 1998a: 245) he has produced in collaboration with Thea Elvsted. It seems that Hedda is in fact herself pregnant, which she does not welcome.

Following the party the drunken Lövborg violently accuses one 'Mademoiselle Diana' of robbing him and subsequently assaults a policeman. Having lost his manuscript and become embroiled in scandal Lövborg tells Hedda he will kill himself. She provides him with one of her father's pistols and exhorts him to do it 'beautifully' (246). But he dies in another scuffle with

Diana, shot in the stomach in unclear circumstances. Hedda had asked him to do it nobly, putting a bullet into his temple. 'Everything I touch seems destined to turn into something mean and farcical' she laments (259). Brack knows that she provided him with the gun, and now Hedda knows she will be subject to sexual blackmail. As Jörgen settles down devotedly with Thea to reconstruct Lövborg's book from her notes, Hedda takes the remaining pistol and shoots herself through the head.

Ibsen's works significantly altered the direction of western drama. Typically it presented troubled middle-class individuals who are engaged in a doomed conflict with a hypocritical and shallow society seeking self-fulfilment. From now on social critique would be even more firmly established as a principal function of the stage.

In *A Doll's House* (1879) Ibsen made a powerful feminist statement in depicting a woman escaping an infantilising marriage but at great cost to herself. *Hedda Gabler* is not so obviously a feminist play. Hedda possesses a Romantic passion for courage for its own sake and believes in the nobility of a 'beautiful' suicide (258). She thinks of Lövborg as the classical hero 'with vine leaves in his hair' (227). Her greatest delight seems to be in firing her father's pistols (198). She seems in fact more of a traditionally masculine Romantic hero. It is true that one reading of the play might suggest that she is a tragic figure because as a woman she is denied the chance of playing the role of the self-destructive Romantic artist. A related **psycho-analytical** interpretation would be that she is unable to shake off her strong identification with her father (hence the importance of the phallic pistols). But *Hedda Gabler* does not challenge one of the most powerful feminist critiques of tragedy, that the whole genre sees women as a problem against which the identity and destiny of the male has to be resolved. There is no challenge to male dominance in this play.

Hedda is nevertheless a powerful female tragic protagonist, whose status is not at all undermined by her spitefulness towards both Thea and her Aunt Juliane (177; 227), diminished by her vindictive destruction of Lövborg's manuscript, or entirely compromised by her ambiguous erotic involvement with the cynical and manipulative Brack. Hedda is one of the great tragic roles for an actress. She is a figure who possesses a thwarted energy and a desire for emotional and sexual fulfilment which it is clear that middle-class nineteenth-century Norwegian society cannot provide. It is not any Aristotelian 'error of judgement' which has placed her in this predicament (see above, p. 17); rather it is the society she lives in at this point in history which offers a woman of her nature no hope of happiness. This is a prime example of what Raymond Williams called the shift in the status of the protagonist 'from hero to victim' in 'liberal' tragedy in the late nineteenth and twentieth centuries (R. Williams 1979: 87). Unlike in the case of, for example, Oedipus or Othello, it is never clear to Hedda or to us exactly what the true causes of her tragedy may be, even if her suicide, shocking as it is, makes dramatic sense. The source seems to lie both in society itself, with its strict limits on a middle-class woman's ambitions and desires, and in Hedda's own mind and the Romantic mythology which haunts it. The idea that the most powerful determinants of human action can be found in structures which lie beneath the surface of what we can superficially observe is a characteristic notion of **modernist** thought (see below, p. 113) emerging here in Ibsen.

For Hedda, suicide at a young age by a pistol shot to the temple has an artistic quality which renders death 'beautiful', but she also describes Lövborg's death as the action of someone who 'has settled accounts with himself. He had the courage to do … what had to be done' (256). First of all it's interesting to note how the language of debt is employed here. In his discussion of Ibsen Raymond Williams also pointed out that debt is in fact 'the significant concept' in these plays (R. Williams 1979: 97). Not only are the Tesmans literally indebted to Aunt Juliane (174), but Hedda's aspirations to individual self-fulfilment are indebted to her past in the society which produced her, which values individualism and yet won't accept how the pursuit of individual fulfilment in a grossly unequal society will have consequences for other people; possessing this 'destructive inheritance' she is trapped in a 'tragic deadlock' (R. Williams 1979: 98) and becomes one of that group of Ibsen's protagonists, who, in Terry Eagleton's account, 'are simply mirror images of the corrupt society they denounce, spiritual versions of the individualism which engendered this unsavoury state of affairs in the first place' (Eagleton 2003: 231).

But Hedda's suicide might also be seen as an act of **existentialist** tragic heroism. The questioning of religious belief in the late nineteenth century led to a search for a new foundation of morality. But, if none can be found, then, perhaps what matters is the authenticity of one's beliefs and actions: the fact that they are willed autonomously by me endows them with value in a world which is absurd. For the Danish existentialist philosopher Søren Kierkegaard (1813–55) there was a God, but his unknowability renders human moral systems empty. We are alone. Tragedy in this play would reside in the protagonist's embrace of death as a necessary cost for the authentic pursuit of a deepest impulse, where an individual idea of beauty or just personal consistency acquires the highest value of all, even greater than life itself. Past tragic heroes such as Antony or Jaffeir might have killed themselves out of a sense of shame, but that emotion is a matter of the protagonists' relationship to the wider community. Hedda's existentialist suicide, on this reading, is what she owes (to use that term again) to herself. But there is also perhaps something inhuman about this. Eagleton calls Hedda's encouragement of Lövborg's suicide 'callous' and goes on reasonably to ask 'how are we to identify such authentic impulses, without public criteria which are themselves an affront to individual uniqueness?' (Eagleton 2003: 231).

Hedda's belief in the beautiful death might also be discussed in psychoanalytical terms: see below, p. 159.

Ibsen was an important part of the transformation in serious theatre in the West at the end of the nineteenth century which would require a new understanding of what tragedy might be. But it would also question whether tragedy itself as a genre had a place in the modern world.

FURTHER READING

Cox (1987) still provides a coherent, comprehensive account of the development of Romantic tragedy. Büchner's writings are gathered together in Matthew Wilson Smith's edition (Büchner 2012). Howarth (1975) is a study of French Romantic drama; Hugo (2004) is a good collection of Victor Hugo's tragedies. For English Romantic tragedy *The Cenci* (1819) stands as a notable example (Shelley 2009). MacFarlane (1994) is very useful on Ibsen. Ibsen's *Ghosts* (1998b) and *The Master Builder* (1998c) have perhaps a more intense tragic vision even than *Hedda Gabler*. The other great Scandinavian tragedian of this period is August Strindberg: *Miss Julie* (Strindberg 2008a) and *The Dance of Death* (Strindberg 2008b) are major works.

5

MODERNISM AND TRAGEDY

CONTEXTS

By the beginning of the twentieth century to live in Europe or
North America was to live in 'modernity'. Major changes in how
people related to the world around them required a new kind of
tragedy: so new that some claimed that tragedy itself could no
longer be written in this new, alienated world.

These major changes had been developing for some time but
came to fruition at the beginning of the twentieth century.
Industrialisation and the mechanisation of agriculture produced
mass migration from the country to the city, where people's lives
no longer followed the rhythms of the seasons or even the sun.
The railway, then the motor vehicle and the aeroplane compressed
distance and space itself. Faith in God became eroded in the cities
and was renounced by many intellectuals. The acquisition of
empires in Africa, Asia, and the Pacific was ostensibly justified by
claims of the superiority of Western societies, but the contact
with the integrity and richness of other cultures also served to
undermine confidence in the ideas that supported that superiority.
Mechanisation and mass production produced by this time a
much higher standard of living for many people, but it was in a
world where the individual woman or man seemed themselves to

be an increasingly insignificant member of a faceless large group. The mobilisation of whole societies into war machines in the two World Wars for the purposes of mass slaughter was perhaps the culmination of this process. In democratic societies anyone could now be a tragic protagonist, at the very time when the specific individual seemed to have less worth.

If in this new way of living people relied on technologies and on systems of trade and commerce whose workings they knew little of, so in the same way influential ways of thinking about humanity itself proposed that what motivated and underlay people's behaviour lay beneath the surface of their own thinking. Charles Darwin (1809–82) showed that humans were the product of an evolutionary process consisting of 'natural selection', not of any **Providential** design. Karl Marx (1818–83) proposed that how we understand and think about the world we live in is produced by the economic system and the 'mode of production' of our society. He also argued that the struggle between workers and those who own the 'means of production' was an inevitable historical process. Sigmund Freud (1856–1939) wrote that beneath our conscious mind lies a whole realm of unacknowledged desires, the subconscious, which we strive to repress to maintain mental equilibrium. The sense of not belonging to oneself or to one's place in the world, of 'alienation', is a crucial part of what we have come to understand as 'modernity', and this alienation from our own lives can be seen as the fundamental tragic situation to be explored in theatrical tragedy. John Orr wrote that tragedy of this period is to be understood as 'tragedies of social alienation' (Orr 1981: xi).

At the end of the nineteenth century 'naturalism' dominated the theatre. New plays were typically set in reproductions of domestic interiors and the characters spoke a language which differed little from that of that spoken the other side of the footlights. This was apparently a rational, no-nonsense, common-sense way of representing the world suited to the values of the middle class who had now largely taken complete possession of the playhouses. In fact it was as meticulously constructed as the less 'realistic' forms of theatre which had preceded it. Twentieth-century tragedy would require new kinds of plays with distinctive new forms. Whether the underlying contradictions and struggles that emerged in human tragedy were depicted as being a matter or economic, psychologically subconscious, or atavistic natural forces, or whether tragedy lay in the uncovering of a total lack of meaning or purpose in human life, a whole range of new dramatic forms emerged in the twentieth century.

ANTON CHEKHOV, *THE CHERRY ORCHARD* (1904)

The Russian dramatist Anton Chekhov (1860–1904) famously protested that his last play, *The Cherry Orchard*, was a 'comedy, even in places a farce' (cited in Loehlin 2010: 148), despite the desire of its first producer (Konstantin Stanislavsky at the Moscow Arts Theatre) to turn it into a tragedy. As with many of his plays, it concerns the condition of the provincial gentry in a Russia that we know was on the verge of cataclysmic change following the 1917 revolution. This class was in fact to be annihilated. From our perspective we can see that only by abstracting the play from history altogether can its tragic nature be denied; and if we do so critics are reduced to banalities, claiming that the play shows that 'this is *the way things happen*, this loose, unplanned serio-comic behaviour, without immediate discernible causes or explanations', and that the play has more to do with 'fumbling and bumbling' than tragedy (Gilman 1995: 240). But what Raymond Williams calls the 'true originality' of Chekhov's drama is how, in a whole society of victims of social change, we see 'an orchestration of responses to a common fate'. In a society where people have ceased to understand their relationships with each other, Chekhov works by 'creating a tragic situation, and inviting us to laugh at it' and at the same time 'creating a ridiculous situation, and making it end in tragic breakdown' (R. Williams 1979: 145, 146).

Chekhov's plays do not tend to feature the dramatic confrontations of pairs of characters which remained a feature of Ibsen's drama, nor do they built to powerful revelations or climaxes. As in *The Cherry Orchard*, groups of characters move on- and off-stage, often, it seems, not really paying full attention to each other, reflecting on the uncertainties and often the emptiness of their lives. In the first act of the play Madame Ranevskaya returns home to her country estate after five years absence with her lover in Paris, whom she has now left. She and her brother have no money left, and the heavily mortgaged estate with its beautiful cherry orchard will now have to be sold to pay their debts. Lopakhin, a successful businessman whose father had been a serf owned by Ranevskaya's father explains how if they clear the land and lease it out for city-dwellers to build summer cottages they can be guaranteed a very good income indeed (ordinary Russian peasants had been their landowners' slaves, in effect, until 1860). But Gayev calls this 'nonsense' and Ranevskaya claims 'I don't understand you' (Chekhov 1988a: 293). Gayev then makes a comic speech to an old bookcase, praising it for its service to the family for more than a hundred years. Lopakhin looks at his watch and leaves. The owners do nothing in the face of calamity and hope a rich relative will come to their aid.

Lopakhin is far from being a money-grubbing boor. His vision of Russia's future, of a land of prosperous 'giants' (314) held back by dishonesty and greed, clashes with the revolutionary, utopian vision of the student Trofimov ('mankind is marching towards a higher truth, a higher happiness'; 339), but the two characters can't help liking each other. Act Three takes the form of a ball where the characters dance with each other, even Ranevskaya with Trofimov (328), as they await news of who has bought the estate at auction. Lopakhin arrives to announce that he has bought it so that he can put his plan into action. Ranevskaya weeps bitterly (334), but in the final act she has come to terms with events and is returning to Paris to live on her great aunt's money until that runs out (342). Throughout the play it is clear that Ranevskaya's adopted daughter Varya has feelings for Lophakhin, and he tells her mother that he will finally propose to her just as they are leaving the house for the last time. But he doesn't seem to find the words when left alone with her, they are interrupted (346) and the moment is gone for ever. When the house is finally locked up everyone has forgotten about the ancient servant Firs, who is left in the house to die, still lamenting that Gayev isn't wearing his winter coat: 'When will these young people learn? (*Mutters something impossible to catch.*) My life's gone by, and it's just as if I'd never lived at all. (*Lies down.*)' (349). At the end of the play all that can be heard is the sound of an axe in the orchard.

John Orr describes *The Cherry Orchard* as a sustained 'tragic *lament* ... It is not the individual persona but the collectivity and their environment which is doomed, and the loss is shared harmoniously in a remarkable statement of human solidarity … It is in the integration of subjective feeling and objective process that Chekhov proves so masterly' (Orr 1981: 74). Orr finds a formal harmony in the play between nostalgia and joyful recollection of the past and a fear for the future carefully juxtaposed. He also finds it in the balance between the antagonistic viewpoints but mutually sympathetic characters of Lopakhin and Trofimov. This is a new kind of tragedy without a protagonist, which foregrounds the effects of economic and social change on a whole community, without pointing a finger of blame. Ranevskaya and Gayev are foolish and even feckless, but she at least is drawn so sympathetically, in many ways, that she seems a glorious anachronism rather than a callous proprietor. The abandonment of Firs to his death can indeed be seen as proof of the heartlessness of this class towards their servants, but whilst serving to concentrate a feeling of tragic loss in the play's final moments the old man's last words show a kind of acceptance of how time has rendered him and his views redundant (he did not approve of his own emancipation; 312). There is no grand passion or emotional climax to the tragedy performed by larger-than-life heroes. It possesses a fluid form and a wide range of characters, some of whom add nothing obvious to the 'plot', such as it is (for example Charlotta the governess). The play has an evenness of tone and a subtle and consistent combination of comedy and pathos. *The Cherry Orchard* is a pervasive lament for a whole community of victims of the rapid changes of capitalist modernity, showing how and why change happens, but showing sympathy and understanding for all concerned.

EUGENE O'NEILL, *MOURNING BECOMES ELECTRA* (1931)

In 1926 the American playwright Eugene O'Neill carried in his pocket a worn copy of Nietzsche's *The Birth of Tragedy* (see above, p. 34). It was a work that had great importance for him, for he regarded tragedy to be 'the meaning of life – and the hope'. He claimed that Greek tragedy was the major influence upon his work (Törnqvist 1998: 19). Many early-twentieth-century writers sought to create new forms of art to reflect what they saw to be the radically new circumstances of modern life. But O'Neill sought to go back to the origins of tragedy, to a place where he thought art and the religious impulse were united, to find a way to talk about an alienated modern world. The English poet T. S. Eliot would attempt the same in his plays *Murder in the Cathedral* (1935) and *The Cocktail Party* (1949). O'Neill went right back to the earliest tragedy of all, Aeschylus's *Oresteia* (see above, p. 10), and to Sophocles' *Electra*, and chose to adapt the story of the ancient trilogy by setting it in what he saw to be a more recent heroic age – the time of the American Civil War (1861–65).

But his problem also was how to reanimate the ancient form in a world lacking the universal religious feeling and mythological basis of Greek drama. When starting work on the play in 1926 O'Neill pondered in his diary 'whether it is possible to get a "modern psychological approximation of Greek sense of fate" into a play intended to move an audience which no longer believes in supernatural retribution' (Bogard 1988: 336). His answer was to structure the play around the working out of the Freudian Oedipus Complex amongst its main characters, replacing the workings of divine justice with the machinations of the neurotic subconscious. In fact O'Neill always denied the Freudian influence on his plays, but **psychoanalysis** was clearly an important part of his life at this time (Bogard 1988: 345). Freud originally sought to find the origins of mental illnesses in events which took place in infancy, before a child could speak. One of his theories was that the future mental equilibrium of an infant male depended upon the child being able to dissociate himself from his sexual feelings towards his mother and his murderous jealousy towards his father, and subsequently to bond with his father. These subconscious, unacknowledged emotions, if never resolved, would remain repressed and re-emerge as neuroses, only glimpsed in dreams and verbal slips. But their presence could be also be detected more generally in myth and literature based on myth: Freud sought validity for his ideas in Sophocles' *Oedipus the King* (see above, p. 118), and even in Shakespeare's *Hamlet* (see above, p. 54; Freud 1953: 264–5).

The Oedipal family in *Mourning Becomes Electra* are called the Mannons. Their tragedy, like that of the House of Atreus in

Aeschylus, is depicted in a trilogy of plays, intended to be performed in a single evening. In the first, *Homecoming*, General Ezra Mannon (Agamemon in myth) is due to return victorious to his New England house (with its Greek-style façade) at the end of the war. His daughter, Lavinia (Electra), has discovered her mother Christine's (Clytemnestra) affair with the sea-captain Adam Brant (in fact her husband's brother's illegitimate son), who has also been courting her. Christine also reveals her hatred of her husband and her indifference to her daughter compared to her love for her son Orin (Orestes), who, when he was born in his father's absence, 'seemed my child, only mine, and I loved him for that!' (O'Neill 1992: 29). Lavinia says she will conceal the affair from Ezra if Christine will not see Brant again, but the lovers conspire to poison Ezra on his return and make it appear to be a heart attack. In his dying moments the General lets his daughter know the truth. In the second part of the trilogy, *The Hunted*, Orin also returns from the war. Christine convinces her mother-besotted son that Lavinia is mad and that Orin should not believe anything she says, but Lavinia subsequently wins him over. After witnessing a meeting aboard Brant's ship between his mother and her lover, Orin shoots Brant dead then makes the murder appear the work of a robber. When she is told this news Christine ignores Orin's plea that they should go away together 'to the South Seas' (109) (a dream-world for them where desires can be liberated) and kills herself. In the final part, *The Haunted*, a year has passed and the siblings have been away in the East. Lavinia now looks like and acts like her mother, Orin his father. They both have had a suitor each since the beginning of the trilogy, but Orin now declares his incestuous love for his sister, seeing their mother in her. She responds by wishing he were dead (150). Orin shoots himself, and Christina, having addressed her suitor Peter in an embrace with the words 'Take me, Adam [Brand]!', she tells Peter he must go away and she will now lock herself for ever in the house 'bound here – to the Mannon dead!' (161), whom she cannot forget.

Chaman Ahuja writes that 'the play has been criticised for its exaggeration, artificiality, improbability, hysterical verbosity, diffusive pretentiousness and melodramatic crudity' (Ahuja 1984: 126). The trilogy is in many ways a failure. The incestuous feelings between Christine and Orin are clumsily presented and the stage directions require the actors' physical appearances to change in a crude way to underline how the repressed desires of the Mannons return through the generations: their faces have to be mask-like to show this (9, 33, 43, 65, 84). Portraits of the Mannon ancestors (and Ezra) also hang threateningly over the interior scenes. These echoes of the classical mask are supplemented by an attempt at a classical chorus of townsfolk who perform no choric function (see above, p. 7) at all, but there is a frequent repetition of an old sea-shanty 'Shenandoah', which portentously announces that the characters are 'bound' (5) to a fate they can't escape. O'Neill sought to achieve drama 'on a plane where outer reality is a mask of true fated reality – unreal realism'(cited in Bogard 1988: 339). O'Neill's modernism strives to show the theoretical 'reality' – here psychoanalytic 'truth' – beneath the 'realism' of appearances, a truth not just for the Mannons. He wrote that 'the interpretations I suggest are such as might have occurred to any author in any time with a deep curiosity about the underlying motives that actuate human interrelationships within the family' (cited in Bogard 1988: 345). But his attempt to replace religious belief at the core of tragedy with 'modern psychological belief' failed in an interesting way. Modern tragedy is possible in a world without religion and accreted myth, but it has to be animated by something more profound than theory, by something with deeper roots in the truth of people's experience than the half-baked Freudianism of O'Neill's trilogy. Robert Icke (see below, p. 170) was to achieve a much more effective reworking of *The Oresteia* in the next century.

FEDERICO GARCIA LORCA, *BLOOD WEDDING* (1933)

Lorca, the young gay poet murdered by fascist paramilitaries during the Spanish Civil War, simply subtitled this play 'tragedy'. Lorca's protagonists are Andalusian peasants caught in a titanic struggle between subconscious, elemental natural forces (themselves conflicted) and the kinship and honour codes of a rural society. Folk song and poetry combine with symbolist theatre and even the classical chorus to produce a form of tragedy at once traditional and modernist.

Even though the inspiration of the story comes from a real murder in Níja in Andalusia in 1928 (Lorca 1989: 1), all but one of Lorca's characters have generic names, and stand for an enduring type or social role; although there are one or two references to twentieth-century life in the play, the setting itself seems outside history, in a static rural community. The Bridegroom wishes to marry a woman who was once courted by Leonardo, a member of the Felix family, whose menfolk had been responsible for the murder of the Bridegroom's father and husband. The Bridegroom's Mother, an embittered and resentful figure throughout the play, has forebodings that the marriage will be disastrous. We discover that Leonardo has been secretly riding over to visit the Bride in the days before the wedding – but they are not sexually involved, and the morning of the wedding they declare that there can be nothing more between them; but in this scene their erotic longing for each other is all too evident. At the wedding feast the Bride is uneasy and distracted as Leonardo stalks the edge of the stage, and at the end of Act Two it is revealed that they have ridden off together on Leonardo's horse. The Bridegroom and his relatives set off in pursuit into a surrealist woodland, inhabited by a chorus of woodcutters, a Moon who speaks an erotic ode to death and an old Beggarwoman – Death herself – who oversees the offstage killing of both Leonardo and the Bridegroom in a knife fight. In the final scene, introduced by a chorus of Fate-like girls winding red wool, the Mother, the Bride and Leonardo's Wife come together to mourn, each alone and resigned to a bleak future.

In a lecture given in Buenos Aires in 1933 Lorca spoke of the importance of the *duende* to his art. A term from the tradition of flamenco dancing, the term encompasses not just the spirit of inspiration, but also the intensity of the moment of live artistic expression in the presence of death, with its 'roots in the dark realm of the unconscious; it is an enemy of reason.' It is unrepeatable, 'like the sea and sky in a storm' (Stanton 1978: 11, 12) and indeed its source lies in nature, the earth itself. Lorca wrote that '*duende* is a power and not an action, a struggle and not a thought … it surges up inside you right from the soles of your feet' (Lorca 1989: 6). Death itself appears in this play, omitted from the cast list in programmes so that the impact on the audience may be the greater (86), and the presence of dark subconscious forces which express the natural desires in tragic conflict with social convention have their expression in the play's bold poetic and theatrical symbolism.

Before Leonardo's first entrance his Mother-in-Law and Wife sing a strange and melancholy lullaby to his child about a horse with a 'frozen mane' and a 'silver dagger' in his eye who would not drink at a stream (39), but needs to be left to run 'through valleys grey/ and mountains green/ to his young /mare's side' (41). Leonardo has just been riding his horse very hard (to visit the bride, it turns out), and he is not enthusiastic about the drink his Wife offers him ('make sure the water's good and cold'; 42). He argues with everyone and leaves, angry. The lullaby concludes the scene: 'sleep, little rose, /the horse /is weeping now' (46). Leonardo, who is associated with his horse all the way through the play, is the stallion unsatisfied by his mate who seeks sexual fulfilment elsewhere. His desires, which he himself fights to repress, emerge in the lullaby's natural symbolism, combining the naturalistic and the subconscious in a traditional art form. Lorca's symbolic method continues, culminating in the arrival on stage of the moon, seeking to illuminate the way for the killers to hunt down and shed the blood of the elopers, in order that the Moon can also achieve some kind of sexual fulfilment: 'already I can feel/ the ashen dust of my valleys stir/ in expectation of its rich fountain/ its shivering spurt' (87). The desire for sexual ecstasy and violent death combine in the play's final image of a knife that 'slices so quick/ through the startled flesh/ and there it stops, at the point/ where, trembling enmeshed/ lies the dark root of the scream' (105). The central symbolic motif of the play is blood, a word that carries the irresolvable internal conflict that is the tragedy: blood is the instinctive, elemental force of sexual passion, but it also stands for the family bonds and which attempt to restrain that passion. Reed Anderson writes, 'that which relates and unites and expresses the force of elemental life becomes a symbol of that which divides, generates antagonism and brings violence and death in human affairs' (Anderson 1984: 101).

Yet Lorca's surprising use of a traditional classical chorus in their original function – to offer the audience possible responses to the action – runs in contradiction to the idea that the play's tragic conflict of monumental forces which crush the protagonists is inevitable. One of the woodcutters who open Act Three does remark that the Bride and Leonardo 'followed the pulse of their blood. What else could they do?', but others suggest that 'they should let them go' because 'the world is wide. There's room for everyone' (82). Even in this static world where each generation repeats the suffering of the previous (68) this moment offers some hope of social change. *Blood Wedding* shows twentieth-century tragedy melding folk tradition, the avant-garde and the classical to express a tragic conflict not different in shape from those of *Antigone* or *Othello* (see above, p. 21 and p. 63) but underwritten by theories of the subconscious. A distinctive dramatic form is no longer the mark of the genuinely tragic.

BERTOLT BRECHT, *MOTHER COURAGE AND HER CHILDREN* (1941)

Mother Courage, writes Peter Thomson, 'is not merely an item in the ongoing catalogue of world drama; it is an attempt to intervene in world history' (Thomson 1997: 12). The socialist playwright Bertolt Brecht was in exile from his home in Nazi Germany in Sweden in 1939 when he began work on the play. His intention was to write an **'epic'** play that, in his own words, had an unambiguous message:

> That in wartime the big profits are not made by little people. That war, which is a continuation of business by other means, makes the human virtues fatal even to their possessors. That no sacrifice is too great for the struggle against war.
>
> (Brecht 1983: xvii)

His intention wasn't to write a tragedy. In 1928 he had written that he was one of those people who 'believe humanity is well on the way to getting rid of the tragic entirely, merely by taking civilizing measures' (Brecht 2015: 43). What he called 'bourgeois' tragedy – middle-class orientated, realist drama – was in fact 'crude and shallow' because it never revealed the 'deeper contexts' (Brecht 2015: 52), the causes of human suffering which we are capable of changing through our own actions. The theatre's job is to produce plays which will enable the audience to see clearly what is wrong with our capitalist society and to take action which will end the unnecessary suffering it produces, not merely mystify capitalism's misery, pain and grief as inevitable parts of the human condition. To mix the conventionally comic with the conventionally tragic (Brecht 2015: 283–4) was just one of his methods to produce political insight in his audience, together with a range of other 'alienation' techniques which aimed to enable the spectator to stand outside the action of the play, to come to understand how and why things happen in it and to see that we are capable of changing society and consequently the nature of the people in it through our own actions. Brecht's critique of tragedy is that it has served as a means of producing assenting emotions which make suffering in a socially unjust world seem inevitable, or part of a metaphysical scheme such as fate, and not part of a historical process.

Yet in this play many audiences and critics have found that Brecht has written a genuine tragedy in spite of himself. In the play's twelve scenes Mother Courage pulls her cart through twelve years of the terrible Thirty Years War (1618–48), a long struggle between Catholic and Protestant European powers. Courage lives in her cart which is also her business, from which she sells whatever she can to the armies as she follows them around. She starts selling to the Swedish Protestant Army, then is taken prisoner by the Catholic forces – whom she carries on selling to – and then, after a truce, returns to the Protestants again. She accompanies the fighting wherever it goes. War, whose destruction produces constant shortages, gives her the business opportunity she needs. As she says (when according to Brecht's scene caption she is 'at the peak of her business career'), 'I won't have you folk spoiling my war for me. I'm told it kills off the weak, but they're a write-off in peacetime too. And war gives its people a better deal' (Brecht 1983: 59).

At the beginning of the play Courage has three children, all by different absent fathers. In Scene One her brave son Eilif is persuaded to sign up for bounty money as she is distracted in selling a belt buckle (a montage effect typical of Brecht's technique). Eilif is praised by his general in Scene Two for robbing peasants of their livestock to feed the army. But when he does the same thing during a truce in Scene Eight he is shot for looting. Courage is kept from the truth by her lover the Cook. Her honest son Swiss Cheese becomes the regimental paymaster. In Scene Three he is captured and threatened by thuggish Catholic soldiers who want him to reveal the whereabouts of the hidden strongbox. Mother Courage seeks to raise the money to pay them off and save her son by mortgaging her cart to the prostitute Yvette. But she is so keen to get a good bargain that Swiss Cheese is killed while she is still haggling. The soldiers bring her son's body to her but she pretends she does not know him to save herself from incrimination. Her daughter Kattrin, who is struck dumb after being abused by a soldier, then later disfigured by another who assaults her, yearns for children. In Scene Eleven she gives her life to raise the alarm to save the vulnerable civilians of a German town from surprise attack, whilst the local peasants co-operate with the attackers in order to save their livestock. In the final scene Mother Courage pays the peasants to bury her daughter and sets off alone to drag her now near-empty cart to follow the war once more.

Between the play's first performance in neutral Zurich in 1941 and its first German performance in post-war Communist East Berlin in 1949 Brecht had to adapt his original script because Courage was receiving audience sympathy which detracted from the desired political impact. He tried to make her purely mercenary attitude even more obvious. In Scene One in the Zurich version Courage was consoling an anxious sergeant while the recruiting officer bought Eilif's freedom. In the Berlin version she is selling him a belt buckle. In Scene Five in 1941 Courage had eventually agreed to tear up some shirts she wanted to sell to provide bandages for wounded civilians. In the 1949 version she has to be physically lifted out of the way, in comic fashion, so that Kattrin and the Chaplain can get to the shirts to help the wounded peasants (49). Yet audiences continued to be moved by Courage's deluded but cunning and clever power to endure and by Kattrin's selfless heroism amidst such barbarism, just the emotional identification that Brecht apparently did not want. In 1950 in Munich he added to the final scene Courage's declaration that she has 'got to get back in business again' as she leaves Kattrin's body to be buried (Schwartz 1978: 318; 87).

But the play's continuing impact upon its audience as a tragedy is not necessarily incompatible with political insight. Brecht wrote in 1952 of the play's ending that:

> many actresses playing Courage find it easier and more congenial to play this final scene simply for its tragedy. This is no service to the playwright. He doesn't want to detract from the tragedy, but there is something that he wants to add: the warning that Courage has learnt *nothing*.
>
> (cited in Schwartz 1978: 321)

What matters is that we learn, even if Courage doesn't. He admits that we can find Courage a tragic figure; but Brecht's real concern is that we see how war is driven by capitalism and find anger in that. Helene Weigel, who played Courage in the 1949 Berlin production and was herself an important interpreter of and collaborator with Brecht, not only strove to 'repel the audience's sympathy' (Thomson 1997: 41) but also to engage with their emotions to show the cost of the choices she has made. When Swiss Cheese's body is brought to her at the end of Scene Three archival photographs show her giving a 'silent scream … her head thrown back as if baying silently to the moon' while her hands are 'scrabbling in the lap of her skirt' (Thomson 1997: 40). George Steiner saw this performance and wrote that 'the shape of the gesture was that of the screaming horse in Picasso's [painting] Guernica. The sound that came out was raw and terrible beyond any description I could give of it' (Steiner 1961: 354). It is the choices Courage has made within the historical moment she lives in which produce tragedy here. She is trapped into shocking self-betrayal but she cannot acknowledge it intellectually, only physically. Her gesture shows this. We can learn from this and choose otherwise. *Mother Courage* shows that tragedy can teach how suffering which is the product of systematic injustice could be ended, rather than be a means of making it seem an inevitable part of the 'human condition'.

GEORGE STEINER AND THE DEATH OF TRAGEDY

In 1961 George Steiner, in a sustained and influential piece of modernist pessimism, argued that it was no longer possible to write genuine tragedy in the modern world. He later defended and developed this view in an essay published in 2008.

In the earlier book Steiner proposed that language itself is no longer capable of depicting human suffering with the freshness and subtlety of the premodern era. He argues that 'the deportation, murder or death in battle of some seventy million men, women and children between 1914 and 1947' has 'demeaned and brutalized language beyond any precedent'. The distortion of language to justify the basest political ends in the modern world has meant that 'words no longer give their full meaning'. Moreover, 'each day we sup our fill of horrors – in the newspaper, on the television screen, or on the radio – and thus we grow insensible to fresh outrage' (Steiner 1961: 313, 315). In these circumstances we no longer have the means to write tragedy with the force and power of, for example, seventeenth-century writers.

Modern literary language can convey the despair or terror of the individual writer, but it will lack the grounding in the shared mythological tradition which enables true tragedy to express the feelings of a culture. Mythologies, Steiner writes, 'have centred the imaginative habits and practices of western civilization' and 'have organized the inner landscape' of individuals. 'Great myths' are 'the speech of the mind when it is in a state of wonder or perception'. When we no longer have an intimate connection with a long-established frame of cultural narratives that made sense of our experiences, even at their most terrible, art loses its power to make sense of that suffering: 'when it is torn loose from the moorings of myth, art tends towards anarchy. It becomes the outward leap of the impassioned but private imagination into a void of meaning' (323, 321).

Modern writers like Eugene O'Neill may try to resuscitate the old myths (see above, p. 117) but are doomed to failure since we live in a scientific, post-mythological age. Or, he writes in 1961, like Bertolt Brecht (see above, p. 123) they may draw on the new mythological narrative of Marxism. But Marxism, like modern Christianity, with their visions of socialist utopia or eternal salvation, is fundamentally anti-tragic (324).

Steiner has only deepened his pessimism over the years. In his later essay he writes that we know we are fallen creatures; we are 'made an unwelcome guest of life, or, at best, a threatened stranger on this hostile or indifferent earth ... There is no welcome to the self. This is what tragedy is about' (Steiner 2008: 30–31). In Greek and Christian myth, just as in Marxist and Freudian thought, there is always 'some distant, dread crime or error' which 'has sentenced man to the ever-renewed cycle of frustration, of individual and collective self-destruction'. 'Authentic tragedy' comes out of the realisation that 'not to have been born is best'. He goes on to argue that this sense that our dwelling in the universe is some sort of error 'presumes that there are non-human agencies hostile or at best wholly indifferent to intrusive man' (Steiner 2008: 32). Without the divine, it is hard to have tragedy. When our culture lost its pervasive religious faith it lost the possibility of tragedy. Even when an atheist writer strives for tragic effect, without God there is no comprehensive, meaningful home from which the tragic expulsion from grace can be measured; it is the absence of that fictional datum which must be invoked to produce tragedy. Steiner quotes the character speaking of God in Samuel Beckett's play *Endgame*: 'The bastard! He doesn't exist!' 'In that non-existence, malign without words', writes Steiner, 'lies the evil and ostracism of man's condition' (Steiner 2008: 37, Beckett 2009: 38).

Steiner also questions the possibility of authentic tragedies in democratic societies. The depiction of extremes of suffering requires 'an aristocracy of suffering, an excellence of pain' (Steiner 2008: 37). While not denying that terror and injustice happen to the mass of humanity, when a tragic protagonist is of elevated political, social or heroic status they are closer to the divine. Their fall is greater and their suffering more intense. When they strive to shape history to their will they are in closer contact with the hostile force which is at the root of tragedy. Steiner quotes the German dramatist Hölderlin, who wrote that 'eminent beings ... stand out like lightning rods whom Olympian bolts both irradiate and scorch' (Steiner 2008: 38). The gods destroy those who seek to approach them in power, but they are illuminated brightly in that moment of destruction. In a society without superior beings there can be no such tragic moment of glory.

In a response to Steiner, Terry Eagleton has pointed out that if we define tragedy so narrowly that only those works of art which admit of no hope whatsoever are the real thing, then not even *The Oresteia* (see above, p. 9) would fit the category. He also spots an incoherence in Steiner's argument that true tragedy expresses the hopeless sense of alienation of the human race on earth: even complete pessimism about the human condition must be founded on the possibility of hope: 'If *Waiting for Godot* [see below, p. 135] is pessimistic, it must be because the idea of Godot's coming must always have been conceivable. What makes for tragedy, often enough is the fact that we can conceive of a more humane condition' (Eagleton 2008: 344). Far from being anti-tragic, moreover, Christianity is built on the idea that divinity can be found in the most lowly of humans – God became a human child. 'It is the lesson of a good deal of tragedy', writes Eagleton, 'that only by an unutterably painful openness to our frailty and finitude – to the material limits of our condition – can we have any hope of transcending it' (Eagleton 2008: 345). This is what King Lear learns on the heath (see above, p. 69), but it is what can also be seen in fate of Willy Loman in Miller's *Death of a Salesman* (see below, p. 132). To claim that the tragedy of the former is greater than the latter because of his social status seems perverse if tragedy is about being genuinely open to the facts of the material circumstances in which we live. In fact, as Edith Hall puts it, 'tragedy can only continue to speak to us in the twenty-first century because it has successfully expanded its scope to include the suffering caused to humanity by economic and social oppression' (Hall 2014: 781).

TENNESSEE WILLIAMS, *A STREETCAR NAMED DESIRE* (1947)

In his book *Tragic Drama and Modern Society*, the critic John Orr proposed that many American writers turned away from socialist ideas as the Cold War developed in the immediate post-war period. Instead, under the influence of **psychoanalysis**, 'the figural stress of the new drama was psychosexual', and it tended to portray 'the conflict between the individual personality and society, where the sexual basis of personal disaffection now received an unprecedented recognition' (Orr 1981: 208). In *A Streetcar Named Desire* the tragic protagonist, Blanche Dubois, is a curiously ambiguous figure. On the one hand she is a manifestation of guilty nostalgia for the elegance of the old South with its archaic 'chivalry' (which, of course, coexisted with slavery, though that is not mentioned), and on the other she is an over-sexed neurotic who cannot live in modern America except as a damaged, deluded and fragile creature desperate for male protection. Blanche is a pitiable, almost embarrassing figure on stage, but she acquires tragic dignity not just in the way in which Williams rather crudely deploys music, sound and lighting effects as grandiose symbolic representations of her inner psychological states. Her status is also realised in the play's unconscious depiction of repressive restraints on women's capacity for self-realisation in mid-twentieth-century America. Blanche may well have something to say about Williams's own homosexual identity, but the play is actually about what happens to women when heterosexual desire becomes painfully distorted in a class-fractured, highly patriarchal society.

Blanche comes to stay with her sister Stella and her husband, Stanley Kowalski, in their cramped New Orleans apartment. She has had to sell off the old family house, Belle Reve ('Beautiful Dream'), and says she is taking a break from her job as an English Literature teacher through exhaustion. Stella is pregnant. Stanley is shown to be violent towards his wife but it is suggested that the sexual potency of the muscular and machismo Stanley keeps Stella in emotional thrall to him (T. Williams 2005: 13). Stanley resents Blanche's presence in his home. Blanche begins an affair with Stanley's poker-playing friend, the timid Mitch. She tells him how she married very young but her husband committed suicide after she found him in bed with another man (57). Stanley discovers that Blanche had to leave the hotel where she was living previously in her home town for her known promiscuity, and in fact that she was dismissed from her school because of an affair with a 17-year-old pupil (60). Stanley confronts Blanche at her birthday tea and presents her with a bus ticket home. Blanche is sick with anxiety, but Stella feels the baby about to arrive and Stanley takes her to hospital. Mitch finally arrives, drunk, late for the party having being told of Blanche's true past. He tries to force himself on her, but is warded off and leaves. But Stanley returns alone from the hospital and rapes her ('All right, let's have some rough-house! … We've had this date with each other from the beginning!'; 81). In the final scene a doctor and a nurse arrive to take Blanche away to a mental hospital; she has suffered a complete mental collapse, and is obsessed with a delusion that a millionaire she once met is about to take her away with him.

The play's first director, Elia Kazan, wrote of Blanche: '*Her problem has to do with her tradition*. Her notion of what a woman should be. She is stuck with this "ideal". It is her. It is her ego' (cited in Orr 1981: 212). Her 'tradition' is the image of patrician Southern gentility, of ladies dependent upon their gentlemen. But Blanche's patrimony, and her position in that class has gone, and consequently, as she tells her sister, 'I've run for protection, Stella, from one leaky roof to another leaky roof – because it was storm – all storm, I was – caught in the centre.' But there is a sexual price to pay for this protection: 'People don't see you – *men* don't – don't even admit your existence unless they're making love to you' (45). Blanche's promiscuity makes her a social outcast in this society but Stanley is driven to distraction by something about her presence until he rapes her, breaking her mind and bringing her under his control, just as his abused wife is kept subservient by his supposed sexual power. In the play's final moments as Stella weeps in '*complete surrender*' to the loss of her sister, Stanley's fingers '*find the opening to her blouse*' (90).

A Streetcar Named Desire is a play where sex is everywhere: in sweating bodies, in its often half-dressed characters, in its many scenes of seduction and flirtation. Sexual desire is presented as an elemental electricity, a vehicle (a streetcar) that carries people to its fated destination. But, to step back and a look at the play from a gendered perspective, Blanche's notion of her 'tradition', of 'what a woman should be' is also that of the whole drama. Sex operates as a function of power. Women only have an identity in this society as sexual possessions of men. Blanche's behaviour acknowledges that, but she falsely clings in her head to an idea, no matter how tawdry, that there is a grace and beauty in the world ('such things as art – as poetry and music'; 41), a notion to which Stanley stands in antithesis. Despite all that is wrong with Blanche's anti-immigrant, class prejudice ('there's even something – sub-human ... something – ape-like about him [Stanley]'; 40), Blanche, with her melodramatic poses and her delight in pseudo-poetic hyperbole ('Why, the Grim Reaper had put up his tent on our doorstep!'; 12), possesses a love of beauty and of a life beyond male sexual power. But this is cancelled out by her own desperate sexual surrender to so many men, reinforced by her dwelling in the residual **ideology** of Southern 'chivalry'. A new ideology rules now, entirely materialist and where male sexual power leaves no room for anything non-material, such as the non-commercial aesthetic. Blanche is caught in an ideological clash which requires her destruction, but in doing so she reveals the truth of her society. It is a kind of Hegelian tragedy in that sense (see above, p. 24)

ARTHUR MILLER, *DEATH OF A SALESMAN* (1949)

Writing in the introduction to his collected plays in 1957, the American dramatist Arthur Miller declared that a play 'ought to help us to know more, and not merely to spend our feelings'. This dig at the classical notion of emotional *catharsis* (see above,

p. 16) is part of a declaration of political intent. Modern tragedy should give us 'a new and heightened consciousness … of causation in the light of known but hitherto inexplicable events'. By these events he meant how people lived in capitalist America, and he wanted to lay bare 'a new concept of relationships between the one and the many and history', showing 'the inexorable, common, pervasive conditions of existence in this time and his hour' (cited in Schwartz 1978: 43) and the political and economic reasons for those conditions. Miller's suspected complicity with communism meant that he had his passport taken away that year and was blacklisted by a committee of Congress, the House Un-American Activities Committee.

Miller did not seek a new form of left-wing theatre as Brecht did (see above, p. 123) in order to write political tragedy. *Death of a Salesman* is a naturalistic play, even if it does employ some expressionist features. The action takes place mostly inside Willy Loman's house in New York. The house on-stage has no exterior walls, leaving a forestage which is used '*as the backyard as well as the locale of all Willy's imaginings and of his city scenes*' (Miller 1961: 7). What is going on inside Willy's memory as well as his imagination is as important as the 'real' action of the play and at times we can see the characters that Willy is apparently hallucinating who remain unseen by the other characters. Willy's psychological disintegration is shown to be part of the same process as his physical and, crucially, economic degradation.

Willy Loman is a travelling salesman in his sixties. Weary and exhausted at the end of his career he can no longer sell the firm's line of products as he drives hundreds of miles over the north-eastern United States. He has been taken off salary and is on commission, so he earns nothing and is kept going by a gift of fifty dollars a week from his neighbour Charley. Willy has two sons. The eldest is Biff, now 34 and hostile to his father. He is a one-time high-school football idol who failed to win a college scholarship and has been drifting through a series of low-paid jobs all over the country. His younger brother Happy works in New York but spends his time womanizing. We see that the reason for Biff's failure to retake a crucial exam is his discovery of Willy's affair with a receptionist in Boston. He knows Willy is 'a fake and he doesn't like anybody around who knows!' (45). On the second day of the play's action Biff fails dismally in one last attempt at getting a loan to start in business and Willy is not only turned down for a desk job in New York but is fired. He is abandoned by his sons in a restaurant as they go off with two women Happy picks up. After a climactic row with Biff Willy kills himself by crashing his car, convinced that the insurance money will set his son up for life ('a guaranteed twenty-thousand-dollar proposition'; 99).

Willy's faith in what Biff calls 'that phony dream' (106) remains undiminished: the idea that 'in the greatest country in the world' (11) anyone who works hard can become rich and successful. Rather, Miller shows how, in Raymond Williams' words:

> Willy Loman is a man who from selling things has passed to selling himself, and has become, in effect, a commodity which like other commodities will at a certain point be discarded by the laws of the economy. He brings tragedy down on himself, not by opposing the lie, but by living it.
>
> (R. Williams 1979: 104)

The semi-imaginary and preposterous figure of Willy's uncle Ben – explorer, entrepreneur, amoral cheat (38) and ideological icon – stands for 'the lie'. There are no heroes struggling against society; all the Lomans are beaten from the start, and if there is a knowledge to be gained, as well as a spending of feeling, it is of the nature of the consumerist society which will consume its consumers (the text of the play is a litany of products and goods). The tragic hero is passive, and shows that we are equally supine as him in our world: as Alfred Schwartz pointed out 'the effect of the new drama [for the audience] is sometimes terror, but more often self-pity' (Schwartz 1978: 50).

If there is a heroic character in the play it is Willy's wife, Linda, who offers unconditional love for her husband and feigns ignorance of his deceits. She is presented as an insightful guide to the characters of others (Happy is a 'philandering bum'; 45), but is also given some of the play's most powerful rhetoric:

> His name was never in the paper. He's not the finest character that ever lived. But he's a human being, and a terrible thing is happening to

him. So attention must be paid. He's not to be allowed to fall into his grave like an old dog. Attention, attention must finally be paid to such a person.

(44)

In a play, however, where women are vain, easy pick-ups (81) or faithless and promiscuous (19), Linda is so saintly as to be almost outside the action of the play, offering perfect love and forgiveness but ultimately without any understanding of what happened to Willy (112). As with so much of premodern drama, *Death of a Salesman* signally fails to offer women agency in tragedy; here they are still either holy wives or sinful lovers, and remain the collateral damage to the fall of the male protagonist.

SAMUEL BECKETT, *WAITING FOR GODOT* (1953)

The sheer scale of human suffering and wickedness manifested in the Second World War and the Holocaust, and the subsequent threat of nuclear destruction, seemed to admonish the power of art to express such horror. The Irish dramatist Samuel Beckett's *Waiting for Godot*, first performed in Paris, is suffused with the bleakness, hunger and devastation of France in the years following 1945. He called the play not a tragedy, but, in its English language version, 'a tragicomedy' since it depicts what some have called a 'post-tragic' world where meaning and value have apparently been lost.

Vladimir and Estragon are two tramps who spend both acts of the play on a bare stage beneath a tree waiting for Godot, who never comes. At the end of each act a boy comes to tell them that Godot will not arrive that evening but will definitely come tomorrow. The two protagonists pass the time squabbling and making up, and in playing out a series of routines, word-games and gags. There is no plot or character development in the conventional sense. In the first act Pozzo visits with his slave Lucky, whom he treats cruelly. In the second act they return but now Pozzo is blind. He cannot recall seeing the two tramps yesterday, nor can anyone recall the past with confidence at any point in the play.

A famous image towards the end of the play seems to sum up its view of human life as brief and meaningless: 'they give birth astride of a grave, the light gleams an instant, then it's night once more' (Beckett 1956: 89). Vladimir puts it even more graphically: 'astride of a grave and a difficult birth. Down in the hole, lingeringly, the grave-digger puts on the forceps' (90–91). Yet the play is full of humour and playfulness, its routines strongly reminiscent of music hall, with Estragon and Vladimir a double-act and Pozzo and Lucky a variety turn. *Waiting for Godot* mocks itself and the audience's expectations of drama ('Nothing happens, nobody comes, nobody goes, it's awful!'; 41), and foregrounds its own self-awareness as fiction: Vladimir even leaves the stage to relieve himself at one point (Estragon reminds him that the toilet is 'end of the corridor, on the left'; 35) The play's **metatheatricality** has been read as underlining its focus on the emptiness of what it is to exist. The French novelist Alain Robbe-Grillet wrote that in this play 'everything happens as if the two tramps were on stage *without having a role*' (cited in Schwartz 1978: 344, original italics). They have to work hard to find something to do to give themselves an existence on stage, a purpose and direction, without any higher meaning or value, and this is the tragedy – and comedy – of our own existence. Our lives are merely a series of games too, waiting for a redemption we know will not arrive. There is no sense of history or politics in this play. Lucky and Pozzo prompt no social commentary; the exploitation, vengefulness and cruelty they display are just grounds for pity. They are mere passers-through of the ahistorical world of the primal suffering of Vladimir and Estragon. When the blind Pozzo falls over and cries for help, Estragon responds with '*We* help *him*?' (79). This is 'the human condition' of the theatre of the absurd, each of us alone in the void having to make sense of the fact of existence.

As Terry Eagleton points out, however, Beckett's work is not devoid of a sense of worth or purpose in life. Even if 'much of the value of his writing lies in the remorseless demystification of what conventionally passes for value' it remains the case that 'gloom implies value quite as much as grandeur does' (Eagleton 2003: 66, 67). Tragedy lies in the play's sense of loss of secure, discernible values, whilst being aware of their necessity; without some sense of human worth there can be no tragedy.

The play's metatheatricality can certainly be read more positively. A more postmodern reading would find purpose in playfulness itself, as a meaningful, self-justifying and joyful activity without having to have some more '**metaphysical**' 'reality' outside itself. It is interesting how Lucky's long and wild 'think' in Act One keeps returning to sport even in the face of death, ending ' … the skull the skull in Connemara in spite of the tennis the skull alas the stones Cunard … ' (45). There are other sources of meaningfulness available. The affection and companionship which Vladimir and Estragon show to each other right through to the end is far from insignificant, it must also be added: they are not existentially alone, they have each other ('we embraced … we were happy … '; 65). There is also a clear Christian subtext in the play, with Vladimir and Estragon standing either side of the bare tree which recalls the cross, explicitly recalling the two thieves crucified alongside Jesus (12). The tree also acquires leaves in the interval, a sure sign, Estragon believes, of the spring and rebirth (66). What they have offered to Godot is also called 'a kind of prayer', but he said 'he couldn't promise anything' (18). They sustain their faith in the coming of Godot even when he doesn't keep his promise. The absence of God does not diminish the need for the certainty his existence would offer. But it would make the world which Beckett depicts all the more tragic. There are no tragic protagonists here, rather a view of all humans seen outside of historical process in an existentially tragic situation: seeking for a meaning beyond themselves that is not available, but paradoxically the more heroic for continuing to seek it in spite of the evidence. Yet, importantly, the lack of certainty about anything in the play leaves open the possibility that meaning, purpose, and redemption may still be available somewhere (Eagleton 2003: 67), even in religion or politics.

The play ends with Estragon's trousers falling down, but he pulls them up, eventually. 'Well? Shall we go?' asks Vladimir. 'Yes, let's go', he replies. '*They do not move*' reads the final stage direction. Ultimately, if *Waiting for Godot* is not a complete tragedy it is because it relishes the absurdity of life with an affirmative theatricality that its own bleak and sardonic detachment doesn't quite succeed in undermining.

RAYMOND WILLIAMS, *MODERN TRAGEDY* (1966; REVISED 1979)

Williams, the son of a Welsh railwayman, was part of the wave of working-class writers and academics who came to prominence in post-war British cultural life. His left-wing politics could not be separated from his analysis of literature and culture, which saw art as the expression of particular historical forces in a society. The experience of tragedy, he wrote, 'commonly attracts the fundamental beliefs and tensions of a period [in history]', and, in the theories which are formulated to explain tragedy at a particular time, 'the shape and set of a particular culture is often deeply realised' (R. Williams 1979: 45).

Williams was hostile to the contemporary idea that an 'accidental' death could not be tragic, that tragedy requires the suffering of an individual to demonstrate some general statement about the nature of human life, often of an ethical nature. But to do this is to shut off understanding of the deeper forces which actually produce suffering:

> The events which are not seen as tragic are deep in the pattern of our own culture: war, famine, work, traffic, politics. To see no ethical content or human agency in such events, or to say that we cannot connect them with general meanings, and especially with permanent and universal meanings, is to admit a strange and particular bankruptcy, which no rhetoric of tragedy can finally hide.
>
> (49)

He rejected Steiner's notion (see above, p. 127) that tragedy requires a wider framework of mythological and religious belief, since this idea robs contemporary suffering of profound significance and reduces it to the accidental. In doing so the underlying general forces – political and economic forces – become insignificant, and ignored in analysis, since the suffering they cause is denied the status of the tragic.

Williams identified two ideas at work in late-nineteenth-century and twentieth-century tragedy and its criticism which he felt had brought the genre to a dead end. First, he saw naturalism (see above, p. 114) as reducing drama to a depiction of a society and a world which was fixed and not subject to human transformation. This clashed with principles of liberalism – the idea of the autonomous individual with an innate right to make free choices about who they want to be. But 'liberal' tragedies such as Miller's *Death of a Salesman* (see above, p. 132) showed the individual to be powerless in the face of the world as it is, portrayed through the lens of naturalism. He also saw **Romanticism** (see above, p. 98) to have resulted in the impasse of the theatre of the absurd, in plays such as Beckett's *Waiting for Godot* (see above, p. 135). Since the roots of Romantic art were in reaction against **Enlightenment** rationalism, the society against which the Romantic hero struggled to find his identity and purpose too easily became seen as rational and as an enemy: 'man could free himself only by rejecting society, by seeing his own deepest activities, in love, in art, in nature, as essentially as social or anti-social' (73). In a tragedy such as *Hedda Gabler* (see above, p. 108) we can see how the internalisation of this feeling leads to self-destruction, and in later works, writes Williams, to nihilism and a death-wish.

Williams saw history, as reflected in tragedy, as a 'long revolution': where the impulse to full human liberation works to fulfil itself in a changing and changeable world where there remains a 'separation between ultimate human values and the social system' (68). This separation is the outcome not of blind fate or evolutionary process, nor of divine diktat, nor of chance. Instead it is the result of the choices of those in power who seek to defend their position and their interests against the mass of people whose suffering is the result of the social system that has been created. But there is nothing simply good or heroic in the struggle to bring about liberation and end so much suffering, principally because that struggle is against other human beings like us, whose rights as humans we have to recognise even in the midst of that struggle. 'In its deepest sense,' writes Williams, 'in our own time ... the common name' of the tragic action 'is revolution' (83). It can, and often does, go wrong and replaces one tyranny with another. Tragedy is the name we give to art that depicts that contradiction in the long revolution towards human emancipation.

In his 1979 edition of *Modern Tragedy* Williams explains how he was thinking of what happened to the Soviet Union after the Russian Revolution of 1917 (212). Surveying the future with some prescience, he finds 'disturbance, shock and loss' in domestic drama (212) to be emerging as a dominant idea to reflect the larger shocks of the coming neoliberal world whose power spreads into all aspects of life, and he also detected a drama based on an absence of communication between people (214). He finds the source of this in Chekhov, locates it in Beckett ('an icy peak of drama in our period'; 214), but he could also have been talking about much late-twentieth-century drama where language often becomes primarily a means of exerting power rather than genuine communication.

FURTHER READING

Orr (1981), Schwartz (1978) and of course R. Williams (1979) remain excellent if different guides to tragedy in the first part of the twentieth century. *The Seagull* (Chekhov 1988b) and *Uncle Vanya* (Chekhov 1988c) stand out as prime examples of the Russian writer's work that can be considered tragic. Gottlieb (2000) offers a range of ideas about Chekhov as a dramatist. O'Neill's *Long Day's Journey into Night* (O'Neill 1991) is another of his characteristic family tragedies. Bogard (1988) and Manheim (1998) provide contextual readings and critical responses to his work. The other two tragedies in Lorca's great rural trilogy are *Yerma* (Lorca 1991a) and *The House of Barnarda Alba* (Lorca

1991b). Delgado (2008) is an excellent critical introduction to his plays. Brecht's writings on theatre are usefully collected together in Silberman *et al.* (2015). Brecht's *Life of Galileo* (Brecht 1996) might also be considered a major tragic work. Thompson and Sacks (2010) is an excellent guide to his work. Tennessee Williams' work notably includes *Cat on a Hot Tin Roof* (T. Williams 2009a) and *The Glass Menagerie* (T. Williams 2009b). Murphy (2014) is an up-to-date critical companion. Arthur Miller's *A View from the Bridge* (Miller 2010) and *All My Sons* (Miller 2009) are plays with a traditional tragic form. Bigsby (2010) offers critical and contextual essays on Miller's work and ideas. All Beckett's plays are collected together in Beckett (2006). Weiss (2012) and Van Hulle (2015) provide comprehensive introductions to his work.

6

THE SURVIVAL OF TRAGEDY

CONTEXTS

In the final third of the twentieth century different ways of looking at literature emerged which reflected larger changes in society and politics. The idea of unchanging, timeless abstract qualities in literary studies was challenged by a new wave of critics who accused these timeless notions of underpinning the power and privilege of existing elites. Tragedy itself came under fire, apparently because in traditional criticism it was associated with the nobility and metaphysical destiny. On one side some took their cue from Brecht's notion that tragedy was a way of making human suffering seem part of an inevitable destiny and thus a means of making social injustice irremediable (see above, p. 123). On the other were those such as George Steiner (see above, p. 127) who claimed that modern tragedy was impossible in a democratic world without gods, myths or noble heroes.

But tragedy from the past continued to be performed again and again in the theatre, and continued to speak to people. Edith Hall pointed out in 2004 that 'more Greek tragedy has been performed in the last thirty years than at any point in history since Greco-Roman antiquity' (Hall 2004: 2). The Greeks and Shakespeare have also been reworked with considerable power and authority, and contemporary dramatists have continued to produce work for which the term tragedy seemed unavoidable. They went beyond the idea in much serious twentieth-century drama that the suffering of human beings alienated by the specific conditions of modern existence could be reduced to analysis of contexts. As Edith Hall, again, remarks, 'a tragedy that made material and economic forces the exclusive causes of the suffering enacted would no longer be tragedy: it would be left-wing agitprop [mere political propaganda]' (Hall 2014: 781) At a time when the proponents of **postmodern** thought denied the existence of truth and saw all culture as a series of competing narratives whose believability depended on the power of the people whose power they validated tragedy continued to work to reveal and explore an absolute inside human consciousness and experience. Contemporary tragedy is no longer the preserve of middle-class white men, either.

Mass suffering on a scale unimaginable in previous ages is in this era presented as spectacle, even as entertainment, available at a click. Terrorists plan and deliver mass killing with an eye to its impact as it appears on our screens. The philosopher Theodor Adorno (see below, p. 152) later partially retracted his claim that it was impossible to produce poetry after the Holocaust, that it was in fact barbaric to attempt to do so (Silverstone 2007: 285), but the point that literature may fail to get any kind of purchase on the scale of such human enormity still resonates. Yet contemporary dramatists such as Edward Bond (see below, p. 144) Howard Barker (see below, p. 147) and Sarah Kane (see below, p. 165) have confronted the nature of violence with an integrity and dramatic power which can only be assimilated to the category of the tragic.

In the late twentieth century the universality of tragedy was also challenged by non-European writers who questioned some of what they saw as the assumptions of Western thought built into traditional notions of the tragic. One is that tragedy is based on the idea of human beings always facing divisions in their understanding of their place in the world. In tragedy 'humans were split from the divine, other human groups, often each other, surely from the material world' (Reiss 2005: 506). In African cultures, claimed Zulu Sofola in 1994, humans are 'endowed with the same Supreme Energy, all creatures are one and the same', with no-one 'perceiv[ing] himself in essence a negative force. It is within this cosmic view of life that the African defines the artist and his role in the society' (cited in Reiss 2005: 507). The great movement of decolonisation in the second half of the twentieth century was the context for this challenge to Western thought, but under the powerful influence of Western culture. In 1973 the Nigerian playwright Wole Soyinka staged a version of Euripides' *Bacchae* (see above, p. 31) at the new National Theatre in London. Soyinka added a chorus of slaves whose adoption of the worship of Dionysus is crucial to the emancipation from the rule of Pentheus, who is characterised as every inch the colonial master (Soyinka 1973: 27). The play does not end in despair and exile for Kadmos and Agave, however, but in a 'prodigious, barbaric banquet' (Soyinka 1973: xi) where all drink the wine, not blood, gushing from the severed head of Pentheus (Soyinka 1973: 97). Dionysian ecstasy stands for the joyful union of all things, natural and human, violent and creative and suffering and conflict is integrated into a natural 'communal feast, a tumultuous celebration of life' (Soyinka 1973: xiii). The *Bacchae* is perhaps the ancient tragedy best suited to such a re-interpretation, and Soyinka's play also shows the influence of contemporary drug counter-culture.

EDWARD BOND, *LEAR* (1971)

The British dramatist Edward Bond has been much concerned with the suffering and violence which he sees as endemic to the way in which our society is constituted. Often seen as an heir to Brecht (see above, p. 123), Bond's take on tragedy has been far from Aristotelian. Rather, he shows the pity and pathos of the tragic situation whilst always exploring both 'the causes of human misery' and the 'sources of human strength' (Bond 2013: 109). Faced with the horrors of late-twentieth-century history, Bond sees the theatre as a special place where people can learn to understand and then to act, to do something to alter what he sees as the cruelty and waste of a militarised and consumerist capitalist society.

Bond's rewriting of Shakespeare's *King Lear* seems to have been a response to Peter Brook's highly influential 1962 production of the play, itself based on Jan Kott's absurdist reading of the tragedy (see above, p. 71). But for Bond, the theatre of the absurd and its principles are 'corrupt' because 'it is inhumanly irresponsible to say that our existence is meaningless' (cited in Gritzner 2015: 57). Bond sees Shakespeare's play as a powerful statement about how a hierarchical society systematically produces suffering which its perpetrators are blind to: except of course the old king after he is reduced to madness and destitution. In Bond's tragedy *Bingo* (1973) the modern dramatist imagines Shakespeare killing himself in despair because his plays – and *King Lear* in particular (Bond 1987a: 4) – could so powerfully depict what was wrong in society but did nothing to change it. Shakespeare's last words are 'was anything done?' (Bond 1987a: 65). Bond's theatre attempts to make its audience understand how and why violence and injustice are produced so that they will indeed try to address what needs to be done.

Bond's Lear is a cruel dictator overthrown by his daughters, Bodice and Fontanelle, but their savage regime disintegrates into civil war. A revolutionary force is led against them by Cordelia, whose husband had sheltered Lear whilst he was on the run after defeat in battle. The daughters' pursuing soldiers had killed her husband and raped her. But Cordelia's successful revolution only produces another tyrannical regime, justifying its brutality by its claim to be creating 'the society you only dream of' (Bond 1983: 85), echoing Lear's own claim at the beginning of the play that the huge defensive wall he is building with slave labour will make his people 'free' (4). Just as Shakespeare's Lear discovers the truth of how 'wretches feel' by being reduced to wretchedness himself, Bond's Lear also undergoes torture, imprisonment, madness and destitution before coming to see the truth of the world he lives in. He passes from a blind madman who speaks of the world in metaphors, riddles and parables to someone who sees things clearly. As he tells Cordelia in their final meeting:

> You sacrifice truth to destroy lies, and you sacrifice life to destroy death
> ... If a god had made the world, might would always be right, that would
> be so wise, we'd be spared so much suffering. But we made the world
> – out of our smallness and weakness. Our lives are awkward and fragile
> and we have only one thing to keep us sane: pity, and the man without

> pity is mad. [...] Your law always does more harm than crime, and your
> morality is a form of violence.
>
> (84–5)

Sanity – reason – is important for Bond. Theatre is a means of making people see their society rationally, with an awareness of our shared vulnerability and fragility. Lear's last action in the play is to begin the task of bringing down the wall, the Iron Curtain-like structure which symbolises fear and political repression for those on either side. He is shot, but his shovel remains upright in the earth (88), as a symbol for action.

In this play Bond makes use of his so-called 'aggro effect' (Spencer 1992: 8) – not seeking to alienate an audience from emotional reaction as Brecht did, but rather to shock them into seeking some understanding of the events through sympathy and reflection (Spencer 1992: 84). This can sometimes be achieved through a grimly tasteless mixture of the farcical and the tragic. When the innocent worker is about to be shot in Act One, Lear doesn't realise that he's standing in the way of the firing squad (4). In an echo of Gloucester's fate in *King Lear*, Bodice and Fontanelle torture Lear's old retainer Warrington by sticking Bodice's knitting needles in his ears ('I'll just jog these in an out a little. Doodee, doodee, doodee, doo'; 15), while a comedy-cockney torturer comments 'Lay off, lady, lay off! 'Oo's killin' 'im, me or you?' (14). The play is full of brutal on-stage violence. Lear's eyes are taken out by a fellow prisoner who is hoping for 'new opportunities' (59) with Cordelia's regime. He blinds the old king with a grotesque machine to render him 'politically ineffective' (62). The same prisoner has just carried out an autopsy on the body of Fontanelle (another echo of the imagery of Shakespeare's Lear, 3.4.33–6). When the organs are brought out of her body, Lear has a moment of insight when he sees how intricately her body is constructed, but can see no trace of the cruelty she displayed alive:

> Where is the beast? The blood is as still as a lake. Where ... ? Where ... ?
> [...] I am astonished. I have never seen anything so beautiful ... If I had
> known this beauty and patience and care, how I would have loved her.
> [...] Did I make this – and destroy it?
>
> (59)

The nastiness of the blood and organs being produced on-stage is intended to have a similar effect upon the audience as on Lear: they and he need to be shocked into understanding that violence and cruelty are the result of the conditions in which we live as a result of people's choices, not because we are naturally brutal to one another. Pity, not fear is at the heart of Bond's tragic method.

Lear is full of allusions to the Cold War, of the contemporary war in Vietnam and elsewhere, and of the looming threat of nuclear annihilation. 'The existence of our species', Bond writes in the play's preface, is 'threatened by its violence' (lvii). Tragedy here has an urgent practical role in placing before us, live, the contradictions and irrationalities of modern political and economic systems and their results. It may be the case, however, as the philosopher Jacques Rancière has suggested, that political art has first to 'rupture the very categories of socio-politically produced meaning' and 'explode the established and totalizing order of meaningfulness' (Gritzner 2015: 85) to be politically effective: the frameworks of ideas through which we understand the world are too powerfully determined by our society to allow an empowering revolutionary insight to be produced on stage or elsewhere. Such a rupturing of these categories is produced by other contemporary dramatists.

HOWARD BARKER, *VICTORY* (1983)

In 1986 Howard Barker published '49 Asides for a Tragic Theatre' in the *Guardian* newspaper. 'We are living', he began, 'the extinction of official socialism. When the opposition loses its politics it must root in art' (Barker 1997: 17). Barker, who had been a left-wing playwright, argued the need for a new revolutionary approach to an oppressive society at a time when capitalism seemed to have triumphed and socialism to have failed. He declared that a new form of tragedy 'is possible again' (Barker 1997: 18). This will be a tragedy which will challenge individuals in its audience to question their deepest values and beliefs and even their identities, free the subconscious and offer a new liberation for some individuals:

> After the tragedy, you are not certain who you are.
> Some people want to grow in their souls. But not all people.
>   Consequently, tragedy is elitist.
> In tragedy, the audience is disunited. It sits alone. It suffers alone.
> In the endless drizzle of false collectivity, tragedy restores pain to the
>   individual.
> Tragedy offends the sensibilities. It drags the unconscious into a
>   public place.
>
> (Barker 1997: 18, 19)

Liz Tomlin (2006: 111) has written persuasively that Barker's new version of tragedy in fact has much in common with romantic tragedy (see above, p. 98), whose protagonists find the society they live in to lack meaningful structure and to have become oppressive towards their inmost needs, or, in Raymond Williams's words, 'society is identified as convention, and convention is the enemy of desire' (R. Williams 1979: 94). As with Romantic tragedy, which strove to respond to the collapse of traditional social hierarchies heralded by the French Revolution, the new tragedy which Barker began to develop in the 1980s is often set in the aftermath of some great social upheaval, and he calls these plays the 'Theatre of Catastrophe'. After a cataclysmic shock to their world-view Barker's tragic protagonists remake themselves, often by performing versions of themselves, by constantly remaking themselves, by enacting their hidden, authentic desires – principally sexual – at whatever cost, and perhaps most of all by seeking out and living pain and even death. Tragedy, claims Barker, has a unique and 'supremely spiritual quality' among 'dramatic forms, and this arises from its abolition of all values in favour of this profoundly healthy engagement with death'. Death has a 'compelling attraction' because it is 'the **Other**, it has a secret domination of most, if not all, lived action' (Lamb 2005: 201). But all values must be abolished for 'health': morality as we know it has no place here. Barker told Charles Lamb that 'you would be wasting your time protesting the immorality of actions in a tragedy – the characters are only what they are, or indeed, precisely what they are, immune from ethical protest. The play is on another ground' (Lamb 2005: 204).

Victory is the first of Barker's plays where the Theatre of Catastrophe emerges fully formed. The defeat of the Commonwealth and the Restoration of the Monarchy in 1660 is the play's setting. Its subtitle is 'Choices in Reaction', with a submerged analogy to the political situation after the triumph of Thatcherism in the 1980s ('a crisis in public morality'; Barker 1997: 52). *Victory*'s protagonist is Susan Bradshaw, the widow of a pious, egalitarian and prominent Puritan who had secured the execution of King Charles I. The new regime of Charles II is digging up the remains of dead regicides for posthumous punishment (as actually happened). The location of Richard Bradshaw's grave is revealed by his loyal secretary Scrope, and his decaying remains are dismembered and put on grim display. Susan Bradshaw sets out to recover and collect together his remains, but this is not an act of piety or homage to her dead husband's ideals. On the contrary, she is embracing the material fact of his death, and her journey into London becomes a series of acts of wanton betrayal, self-humiliation and abasement. She now is disgusted by her husband's sober wisdom ('forever exhibiting his mind … dirty thing it was, great monster of a mind so flashed and brazenly dangling'; Barker 1990: 152). She wants to open herself promiscuously to all experiences of any kind, as she tells the King's mistress Devonshire:

> Yes means no resistance. Yes means going with the current. Yes means lying down when it rains and standing when it is sunny. Yes urge. Yes womb. Yes power. I lived with a man whose no was in the middle of his heart, whose no kept him thin as a bone and stole the juices from him.

(174)

Bradshaw strangely inflames a Cavalier soldier, Ball, with desire. He pursues her and she acquiesces in her rape by him. Afterwards, '*by a great effort of will she assumes exactly the posture she occupied before his arrival*' (176 stage direction). She then lets her companion Scrope have sex with her immediately afterwards. In London she meets the poet Milton, of whom she used to be in awe, and slaps him in the face. She offers no reason beyond 'Listen, if you knew how it mattered I could do that! … I have broken myself into pieces to do this … ' (182). She becomes Devonshire's servant by persuading her to cut the income of all the other servants in order to pay her wages (184).

King Charles forces the pregnant Devonshire to marry the banker Hambro. At the banquet he offers as a wedding gift the mutilated figure of Scrope, with his lips cut off for blasphemy, and with a massive copy of Mr Bradshaw's utopian book *Harmonia Britannica* hanging from his neck. Scrope struggles to cry 'long liff the atheist re-hub-lic!' but Bradshaw calls him an 'idiot' who 'should be nailed to a board' (191). Barker has explicitly stated his intention here:

> It is a non-Utopian art which pits cruelty against pity and recognises their co-existence in the guilty and innocent alike. Who could take sides when the court of Charles II draws the audience into a conspiracy of his wit rather than into indignation at the fate of a decent man. It is indeed difficult to state whether any character in a Catastrophic play commits a bad act, so complex is the state of emotion which surrounds it.
>
> (Barker 1997: 122)

I have to confess that was not my response when I saw this play performed. Ball, angry that the King has put himself in the hands of bankers like Hambro, gatecrashes the wedding feast in disguise and kills Hambro. Devonshire miscarries. Charles produces Richard Bradshaw's head, which he has played with earlier in the play, and makes it appear to drink Hambro's blood. When the king falls asleep Bradshaw steals the head, and on her way out is beaten up by one of Devonshire's angry servants ('*She utters no sound*'; 192 stage direction) Earlier she had recovered most of the rest of his rotting, blackened remains ('Bradshaw was an African. I never stripped in daylight, nor him neither. How was I to know he was an African?'; 183). The play ends with Bradshaw returning to her burnt out house, her husband's remains in a bag, carrying Ball's child, who accompanies her, tongueless and broken by torture. She meets her daughter there who has learnt Latin to read *Harmonia Britannica*. She scorns her: 'Latin? What's that?' (195). She puts her arm round Ball and takes him into the ruins.

Bradshaw's conduct can be read as the play's:

> literally revolutionary impulse and emphasis on constant demolition and self-overcoming, regeneration through destruction, renewal of essence through the breaking of all forms, as the only means by which to pursue, represent or experience briefly, the truth: such is the nature of existential victory.
>
> (Rabey 1989: 134)

Sean Carney identifies Bradshaw's creed differently, as a Nietzschean (see above, p. 34) anti-philosophy which asserts that cruelty 'is at the heart of human existence' and 'pain and loss' its bedrock. In refusing to feel guilt for cruelty and betrayal she opens herself to an authentic experience of pain, breaking the socially constructed concepts that currently give meaning to human existence (Carney 2013: 89). This embracing of pain and personal fragmentation in order to grasp, even if only momentarily, individual authenticity and truth, is the nature of tragedy for Barker: 'Barker locates the possibility of authentic individual experience in the realm of the tragic, which he considers to be sufficiently enigmatic and powerful enough to act as a counterforce against the dominant liberal-humanist ideology of mass culture' (Gritzner 2008: 332). Or of all shared culture, perhaps.

Barker's version of tragedy presents the art form as a unique space where heroic individuals can experience the decentred, fragmented nature of their authentic selves, and not only on the stage. Rabey considers that 'his audiences are offered the chance to participate in, and extend the processes depicted in the plays' (Rabey 1989: 138). Liz Tomlin identifies a Nietzschean 'artist-tyrant' emerging here. The drive for the self-realisation of the tragic protagonist cannot but have consequences for others, and we are left with an 'ethical rationalisation of the cruelty of Barker's philosophy, or a denial of the political consequences of his protagonists' amoral drive for self-determination': the reinstatement of an aristocracy living beyond the moral code that applies to rest of us (Tomlin 2006: 120–21).

ADORNO AND TRAGEDY

The nineteenth-century German philosopher Hegel wrote about tragedy in the context of his belief that humanity was progressing towards a condition of ultimate freedom (see above, p. 24). But what if there has been no progress? Or even the reverse? For Theodor Adorno (1903–69) the horrors of the twentieth century, for which the Holocaust stood as the most appalling and extreme example, barbarism, not emancipation, has been the result of '**Enlightenment**' (see above, p. 139) thinking. For Adorno, the 'instrumental reason' (Jarvis 1998: 14) which constitutes our relationship with the world and with each other in the modern world has stripped the world of 'enchantment' and robbed us of any individual identity. Everything, especially including our sense of ourselves, has become damaged by Enlightenment rationality, which imposes on experience the idea that everything is knowable, categorisable and ultimately fully exchangeable. In the modern word everything is turned into a commodity for purchase and exchange; previously human capacities and practices are now 'reified', turned into alienated, self-directing autonomous forces existing as things in their own right (Jarvis 1998: 8, 53). In a so-called 'free' world genuine human potential and freedom is strictly limited. Tragedy, which deals with the individual subject in conflict with the intractable reality of suffering and death decays in such circumstances; there is no sense in 'late-capitalist' modernity of there being what Steiner called 'the inexplicable and destructive forces that lie "outside" us and yet are very close' (Steiner 1961: 128), and which are necessary to a sense of the tragic. Instead the creative products of our 'administered' society are the output of the dominant and controlling 'culture industry' (Jarvis 1998: 72ff.) which offer an illusion of reconciliation and harmony, silencing the anguish and pain which is the hidden reality of social alienation and damaged subjectivity. Everything in experience must have a 'meaning'.

Yet Adorno believed that works of art, and especially modernist works can possess an independence from this world which is precariously achieved since works of art still remain of this world. But through their form, which distinguishes them from other objects or events, artworks achieve a non-instrumentality: they exist to be themselves, and their relationship to the world is one of 'semblance': they are physically of the world but not of the world because they represent it in some sense (Gritzner 2015: 4). As artworks they are not identical with anything else and so point intriguingly to the 'otherness' that lies beyond the totalising, instrumental reason inherent in our culture, something which it seeks to 'disenchant': the Lacanian Real which is what 'hard core' tragedy (see below, p. 159) has always confronted; the meaningless abyss of death itself and the suffering whose visceral truth late-capitalist modernity wishes to render explicable and thus consolable (whilst rendering 'natural' the inequalities of power central to so much suffering). Yet still the artwork remains the product of its own society and culture, and so does our consciousness which apprehends it.

Modernist and expressionist works of art which draw attention to the difficulty of adequately expressing the nature of modern experience by the obliqueness of their very form – in the theatre the rejection of **naturalism**, for example – also draw attention to the suffering which is rationalised by 'culture industry' art. Although Adorno called tragedy in its traditional forms 'redundant', his concern with the power of art to point to the negative beyond what is represented is precisely germane to the tragic. Karoline Gritzner argues that Adorno's ideas in fact offer an understanding of contemporary tragedy, calling as they do for art which is a 'counterpoint and critique of this ideologically distorted reality, in which culture is constructed as a façade that conceals [in Adorno's words] "the accumulated, speechless pain"', 'an art that wears the colour black' (Gritzner 2015: 169). In this way the theatre of writers such as Howard Barker and Sarah Kane, for example (and also works such as Caryl Churchill's *The Skriker*), in their formal strategies offer just such a counterpoint and critique (Gritzner 2015: 18): in Barker the idea of a coherent, undamaged subjectivity is absent in those characters who reject reason for authentic expression of desire; in *Blasted* and in *The Skriker* time and place and 'reality' are bent and fractured in a context of fear, suffering and death. In addressing intractable extremes of experience tragedy, in the past, and now in its contemporary form, possesses a unique value which also points beyond itself. As Gritzner puts it:

> Tragedy has the power to express the enigmatic and incommensurable substance of human existence – it brings us closer to the abyss of the mind and, using one of Adorno's favourite concepts, therein lies tragedy's aesthetic 'truth value': by expressing the many manifestations of subjective suffering, it establishes a critique of objective reality. In tragedy, suffering constitutes the expressive reality of the individual and ... compromise or remorse do not compensate for pain and anxiety. Tragedy brings a suspension of the rational principle and there lies its paradoxical power to negate, whilst revealing, the instrumental rationalisation of the world.
>
> (Gritzner 2015: 170)

On this account Kushner's *Angels in America* perhaps pulls its tragic punch by employing the radical form of British tragedies but resolving itself with an ending which is too Hollywood (see below, p. 155).

The postmodern attempt to declare tragedy dead or reactionary, an art form dependent on supernatural powers, or on individuals with fixed human natures and on discredited meta-narratives such as those of innate class superiority, or of religion, fails because tragedy, especially in these forms, addresses realities of death and suffering whose significance cannot be playfully parodied; it addresses a gross, pervasive and currently inescapable constraint on human freedom and joy which cannot be portrayed as an illusion where **subjectivity** itself is a mere effect of language. For Adorno, our relationship to the work of art, to tragic art, is at an important level non-conceptual, a bodily, physical apprehension (Gritzner 2015: 163); it is fleetingly outside the web of language in which the postmodernists claim we are trapped and dissolved. In Edward Bond's words it is 'the world we prove real by dying in it' (Bond 1983: lxvi).

TONY KUSHNER, *ANGELS IN AMERICA* (1991–2)

Kushner's two-part epic, consisting of *Millennium Approaches* (1991) and *Perestroika* (1992), is a remarkable vision of the United States in the mid-1980s on the verge of apocalypse. Not the feared apocalypse of nuclear holocaust, since the end of that decade saw the collapse of the USSR and the end of the Cold War, but apocalypse in the true sense of the word, where the hidden truth of the hopeful new Millennium may be revealed. Kushner's prophet of the new age is a gay New York AIDS victim, Prior Walter, and his status is conferred by the visit of an angel. Yet the play also offers a tragic vision of a world on the verge of environmental catastrophe, watched over by awesomely spectacular but ultimately powerless angels, who can only observe the fate of humanity in a world where God has departed (He left on the day of the 1906 San Francisco earthquake), probably never to return (Kushner 1995: 177).

The action of the play concerns three relationships, which all end with one partner leaving irrevocably. Louis abandons his lover Prior when he discloses he has the disease, and is not accepted back by the prophet at the end of the play. Joe is a legal official, a Mormon, and a repressed homosexual who leaves his agoraphobic wife, Harper, to have an affair with Louis. But Louis rejects him when his complicity in reactionary court judgements under Reagan's presidency are revealed, even though he has turned down a well-paid promotion as a minion of the evil political fixer (and also closet-gay) Roy Cohn. There is a truth to be revealed inside Prior, Joe and Roy, and what is hidden is either deadly (for Prior and for Roy, who is also infected) or emancipating (Joe). All face apocalypse. Harper will not have Joe back but jets off to a new life in San Francisco with his credit card (273, 275). The abandonment of the lovers echoes the abandonment of the world by God, like the *deus absconditus* of Racine's seventeenth-century French tragedies (see above, p. 89). *Angels in America* also evokes classical tragedy in other obvious ways. The Valium-addicted and raving but insightful Harper echoes *King Lear*'s wise Fool (see above, p. 67) or the raging prophetess Cassandra in Aeschylus' *Agamemnon* (see above, p. 9). Prior is losing his sight but his understanding of what is happening in the play is apparently most prescient (like Tiresias in Sophocles' Theban tragedies, or even *King Lear*'s Gloucester, see above, pp. 18, 21 and 68) (Savran 1997: 15). But the supernatural element here is derived from both Mormonism and the writing of the German scholar Walter Benjamin.

Mormons believe that an angel came down to give a revelation to their founder, the prophet Joseph Smith. He led his followers, a persecuted minority in the 1830s and 1840s (Savran 1997: 25) on a journey west to find their promised land in Utah. Here a theatrically spectacular and sexually thrilling angel brings a book of revelation to the prophet Prior, but he returns it when he visits heaven: the angels, terrified by the speed and energy of human activity, want an end to movement, migration, to mixing (178–9), but Prior protests 'we can't just stop. We're not rocks – progress, migration, motion is … modernity. It's *animate*, it's what living things do. We desire' (263–4). But Prior's surname deliberately also evokes Walter Benjamin's image of the angel of history (Savran 1997:18):

> His face is turned towards the past. Where we perceive a chain of events, he sees one single catastrophe which keeps piling wreckage at his feet. The angel would like to stay, to awaken the dead, and make whole what has been smashed. But a storm is blowing from Paradise; it has got caught in his wings with such violence that the angel can no longer close them. The storm irresistibly propels him into the future to which his back is turned, while the pile of debris before him grows skyward. This storm is what we call progress.
>
> (Benjamin 1999: 249)

The idea that history is benignly progressing towards utopia is rejected by Benjamin. Instead a sudden explosion is needed to arrest time, a moment when a new dispensation arrives to change the course of human suffering. And as the ghost of the communist spy Ethel Rosenberg declares to Roy Cohn, 'history is about to crack wide open. Millennium approaches' (118). If it is about to crack open, Kushner's angels, like Benjamin's, are mere horrified observers of piled-up human destruction. Their celestial headquarters is crammed with antique technology, and when Prior visits they are listening to a BBC news broadcast about the Chernobyl nuclear disaster on a failing 1940s radio (260). The disaster is still two months away, but there is nothing they can do to stop it, or even to fix their radio. The callous angel Antarctica blames humanity for its own fate, and weeps for 'the irremediable wastage of Fossil Fuels, Old Blood of the Globe spilled wantonly or burnt and jettisoned onto the crystal air' (262). There is of course something highly camp and self-consciously theatrical about these angels; Kushner says the wires on which they fly should be visible (11; Wallace 2007: 86), and Prior greets his first encounter with arch comment '*Very* Steven Spielberg' (124). The tragic destruction of the environment with which the earth is faced turns out for the prophet Prior to be so last-century. He simply wants 'more life'. If God does return, 'take Him to Court. He walked out on us. He ought to pay' (267). The abandonment of humanity by God and the loss of the 'enchantment' (see below, p. 152) of the world is reduced to a one-liner both about stereotypical New Yorkers and about Prior's own relationship with Louis.

The idea of the Millennium has been an important part of evangelical Christian thinking in the US. The apocalypse envisaged is not Cold War nuclear destruction, but the 'rapture' when the saved will be flown up to heaven leaving the sinners to suffer horror on earth before Christ rules for a thousand years (the 'Millennium'). As Harper flies west to San Francisco at the end of the play, she tells how she dreamt that she saw the souls of the dead rising up from the earth below: 'and the souls of these departed joined hands, clasped ankles and formed a web, a great net of souls, and the souls were three-atom oxygen molecules, the stuff of ozone, and the outer rim absorbed them, and was repaired' (275). Her fantasy is that religious experience will save the planet. San Francisco in ruins is heaven, and also the site of the 'bath houses' where AIDS was supposedly widely spread through sexual contact in the 1980s. Amidst all the play's paradoxes, however, the idea remains that a new religious experience will provide the rupture with history, and the Millennial world will in fact offer not political utopia, but sexual emancipation and unending delight (Joe's prim Mormon mother Hannah has '*an enormous orgasm*' (252) when she meets an angel). The end of communism, the moment the historian Francis Fukuyama in 1989 notoriously called 'the end of history' (Garner 1997: 178) ushers in a post-political, post-systems world of emancipated, autonomous liberal individuals underpinned by religious experience, however self-consciously ironised. The title of the second play, *Perestroika*, is the Russian word for 'reconstruction' and was the policy programme of the Soviet Union's last leader, Mikhail Gorbachev, as he sought vainly to reorder his country's crumbling command economy in the 1980s. The play's satirical prologue features a speech by the despairing Aleksii Antidilluvianovich Prelapsarianov, 'the World's oldest living Bolshevik', who facing *perestroika* proclaims that there can be no change unless backed by '*Theory*' (147). But now the ghost of atheist, theory-supported communism makes its peace with its most implacable enemy when the spectral Ethel Rosenberg, alongside Louis, recites the Kaddish, the Jewish prayer for the dead over Roy's corpse (256–57). This is 'fucking miraculous', according to Louis (257).

The play's final scene, set in front of the angel-topped Bethesda Fountain in Central Park takes place in 1990. Prior has survived on the stolen stash of illicitly acquired AZT drugs taken from the dead Roy's locker. A Jew (Louis), an African American (Belize) and a Mormon (Hannah) argue happily, discussing politics, miracles and the end of theory (278). Prior is above all this, and tells the audience 'you are fabulous creatures, each and every one. And I bless you: *More Life*. The Great Work Begins' (280). This utopia turns out to be the idealised world of American liberal democracy; David Savran describes it as politics 'subordinated to utopian fantasies of harmony in diversity, of one nation under a derelict God' (Savran 1997: 31). It's an apparently anti-tragic ending whose homely self-esteem building rhetoric hides the shallowness of the messianic 'message', hiding the continuing power of Roy Cohn's neoliberal friends and the environmental catastrophe lamented by the angels. The disease remains within the system.

LACAN AND TRAGEDY

If every aspect of human activity can be explained by the social, political and economic forces which shape us – an assumption common in late-twentieth-century thinking – what place is there for the tragic? This challenge can found in the different critical approaches of both George Steiner (see above, p. 127) and Bertolt Brecht (see above, p. 123). The French psychoanalyst Jacques Lacan (1901–81) developed the work of Freud to include just those historical forces in his explanation of the constitution of the human mind; he said that the language which shapes our thought and identity is a direct product of those forces (Bertens 2001: 162). But his account of how we are formed as **subjects** also requires the presence of a dark presence beyond language, something literally ineffable. Some literary critics have seen the existence of this Lacanian 'Real', as he called it, as 'the most profound plane of our experience', into which 'it is tragedy's great function throughout history ... to induct human beings' (Fernie 2007: 34).

For Lacan the infant (literally, the non-speaking child) begins by experiencing a sequence of images, sounds and sensations in their consciousness ('the Imaginary') which cannot be ordered into meaning until she or he enters the 'Symbolic realm', by learning a language not their own but that of the society they are born into, a language already inscribed with all the power relations and inequalities of that society. For ever after we feel a kind of lack for what we have lost in entering this realm: oneness with the mother's body, or a feeling of wholeness, of 'undifferentiated being' (Bertens 2001: 162); we feel a deep-seated longing which cannot be fulfilled but which attaches itself to temporary, symbolic substitutes. Terry Eagleton writes of Lacan as a 'tragic philosopher', for in this process of joining the 'symbolic realm' 'the subject risks losing itself in the very medium which it allows to emerge into being' (Eagleton 2003: 200). But the realm of language cannot allow us access to the 'Real', the actual world beyond the tokens we use the represent it: the connection between language and the reality it represents is arbitrary, and language itself is socially constructed, not a clear pane of glass through which we can access the world: 'the act of perceiving reality filters it through consciousness where it enters into the psychological logic of the Imaginary and the Symbolic. The Real ... *resists* symbolisation' (A. Roberts 2000: 66). But if the Real resists being represented in language there are moments in tragic art where its invocation is the stuff of tragedy itself.

In his lectures on Sophocles' *Antigone* (see above, p. 21), Lacan focuses on Antigone's decision to bury her brother Polynices' body, even though he was a traitor who wanted to destroy their city, and in full knowledge of the death sentence such an act will bring. She asserts the uniqueness of her bond to this individual, a desire which cannot be expressed, an act which 'affirms the unique value of his being without reference to any content, to whatever good or evil Polynices may have done, or to whatever he may be subjected to. That unique value involved is essentially one of language.' Consequently 'it is nothing more than the break that the very presence of language inaugurates in the life of man' (Lacan 1992: 279). In an act which necessarily entails her death she goes beyond language and all it tells her to confront the Real, the emptiness, than which there is nothing more real. Death isn't a linguistic or social construct. But the Real is far more than death. The 'perfected self' which Antigone achieves here 'is blank, perfectly disintricated from social and historical life. It's therefore extremely difficult to distinguish from the state of death, to which Antigone accordingly runs as a bride' (Fernie 2007: 37). But to 'disintricate' oneself from the historical, the social, from language itself through an action (which entails suffering and even death) is nevertheless an escape from the bonds of the symbolic realm into a new freedom; it can be 'the founding gesture of a new order and a new self. Tragedy therefore teems with a strange, undetermined incipience' (Fernie 2007: 38). Lacan's ideas can be seen to offer an insight into the tragic protagonists of Howard Barker's Theatre of Catastrophe (see above, p. 148) as they seek to define themselves by acts driven by pure desire, often violent acts. Tragedy on this account is not 'metaphysical in as much as its locus is the sphere of bodily disintegration and death. And yet degradation turns out paradoxically to harbour another, transcendent life' (Fernie 2007: 38–9). In the theatre of Sarah Kane just such a transcendence can be seen to emerge from horrific suffering (see below, p. 165).

Terry Eagleton identifies the sense of loss which is the price of entry into the unavoidable Symbolic realm with death itself. To embrace that desire is 'to grasp that which defines you, that death is what makes one's life real. This, then, which Lacan bluntly terms the reality of the human condition, is a tragic imperative, exhorting the subject to an affirmation which can only arise from embracing its own finitude' (Eagleton 2003: 233). Antigone 'comes to symbolise the sublimity of desire', as 'her loving fidelity to the Real rips through the symbolic order and moves unswervingly towards death' (Eagleton 2003: 234). It is not a simple death-wish; it is rather that absolute, liberating self-integrity can only be realised through an act which embraces death. That is the nature of tragedy for Lacan. For Eagleton, however, the outcast tragic protagonist who rejects the values of their world and suffers destruction can also provide a liberating, actually revolutionary social insight:

> Rebuffing the claims of the symbolic order ... the ... Lears,
> Oedipuses and Antigones ... inaugurate a revolutionary ethics

by their death-dealing, heroically tenacious commitment to another form of truth altogether, a truth which discloses the negativity of the subject rather than lamenting a positive regime, and which figures for Jacques Lacan as the terrifying abyss of the Thing or the Real. Such figures represent a truth which the system must suppress in order to function; yet since they therefore have the least investment in it as a social group, they also have the strange hallowed power to transform it. They incarnate the inner contradictions of the social order, and so symbolize its failure in their own.

(Eagleton 2003: 280)

Eagleton could also be talking about Edward Bond's Lear (see above, p. 144), or the complex, fragmented, degrading 'unrealistic' experiences of the protagonists of Kane's *Blasted* or Churchill's *The Skriker* (see below), or other modern tragedies where, standing outside the meaning-making framework of the symbolic order, they embody a glimpse of a more liberated, authentic, fulfilling existence only encountered through the suffering produced by the society whose values and beliefs that symbolic order expresses and enforces.

CARYL CHURCHILL, *THE SKRIKER* (1994)

Churchill's plays are not shy of confronting the most threatening and serious questions confronting humanity today from a perspective grounded in ordinary life. *Love and Information* (2012), for example, considers the consequences for human identity and emotion in a world of information overload in the face of the digital panopticon; *Escaped Alone* (2016) sees impending human cataclysm from the perspective of four ordinary women sitting in a garden. Faced with 'rational' human domination of the planet, the issue may be whether tragedy remains a possible artistic response in the face of our fear of what human beings can wreak upon each other and upon the environment, when we have created 'a completely secularized, reified, rationalized human world, where humanity is in charge of its own destiny ... There is no crime we are not capable of, and no crime that cannot be bested with a worse deed' (Carney 2013: 223).

But, in *The Skriker*, Churchill does write a modern revenge tragedy: here the vengeance is of nature, represented by the world of sprites and fairies, against what humanity has done to it. The Skriker is a shape-shifting fury (see above, p. 11) who appears in the lives of two young women in their late teens: Josie, who begins the play in a mental hospital having killed her 10-day-old baby, and her pregnant friend Lily. In a long opening soliloquy spoken in the distinctive jumpy, associative style of the Skriker as herself, she talks of how enchantment has been driven from the rationalist world. Once people would leave gifts to appease the sprites but now humans have steadily poisoned the very nature from which fairies spring. The Skriker will have her revenge:

> They used to leave cream in a sorcerer's apprentice. Gave the brownie a pair of trousers to wear have you gone? Now they hate us and hurt hurtle faster and master. They poison me in my rivers of blood poisoning makes my arm swelter ... Revengeance is gold mine, sweet. Fe fi fo fumbledown ...
>
> (Churchill 1998a: 246)

She befriends each woman in turn, granting wishes as she changes shape throughout the play. The Skriker appears as a brash American in a bar, as a street beggar, as part of the fabric of a sofa, as a needy child and as Lily's older lover. She makes money fall out of Lily's mouth at one point, and toads out of Josie's at another. On stage at the same time, and with no apparent connection to the story of Josie and Lily, there appears a variety of fairies, monsters and hobgoblins from British folklore. They haunt the stage, accompanied by humans who dance with them, leave them presents or just long to see them; these encounters sometimes end in bloodshed. Their actions and meaning stand beyond our comprehension; they are impersonal and inhuman.

The Skriker takes Josie down to the underworld where she dances with these creatures. When she returns no time has passed. In a final attempt to make the Skriker 'leave everyone else alone' (289) and 'make the fury better' (290) Lily also agrees to go down herself to the underworld, but in a powerfully realised but simple piece of theatre she returns in the future to a dark and devastated planet, populated only by '*an old woman and a deformed girl*'. The old woman is Lily's granddaughter, and '*the girl bellows wordless rage at Lily*'. The Skriker speaks her accusation of her ancestors: 'they were stupid stupefied stewpotbellied not evil weevil devil take the hindmost of them anyway' (290). Lily takes some food from the old woman, and the enchanted 'Passerby', who has been dancing throughout the play, stops dancing. It is the end.

What does the Skriker represent? Critics differ. For Elin Diamond, 'Churchill's Skriker is the unassimilable it, the impersonal materiality of the natural world that human beings exploit and poison but cannot control' (Diamond 2014: 756). Nonhuman life has an agency which is figured here through folklore characters, and especially through the playful but dangerous wish-granting figure of the fairy. But in this play, although the malevolent fairy delights in human catastrophe ('I'm going to be around when the world as we know it ends ... I like a pileup on the motorway. I like the kind of war we're having lately. I like snuff movies. But this is going to be the big one'; 283), she is herself dying ('You people are killing me, do you know that? I am sick, I am a sick woman'; 256). Diamond calls this state of affairs 'tragic materialism, a condition of suffering that is acute, impersonal and unredeemable' (Diamond 2014: 754). This is 'posthuman' tragedy because it sees the material world as having agency but also suffering in itself beyond whatever self-centred meaning humans project onto it. It is tragic for Diamond because she finds in the play a force directly analogous to that found by George Steiner (see above, p. 127) in Greek and early modern tragedy: 'a hidden or malevolent God, blind fate, the solicitations of hell ... it mocks us and destroys us' (Steiner 1961: 9; cited in Diamond 2014: 756). Josie and Lily cannot leave the Skriker alone, and compete for her attention and reject her by turns; but it is a relationship of mutually assured destruction.

Candice Amich sees the Skriker as 'the agent of space-time compression' in a globalised, digitised world (Amich 2007: 400), in which case the humans are locked in a tragic, Faustian (see above, p. 51) bargain with postmodern capitalism. For Sean Carney the Skriker is a dramatised version of our damaged psychological relationship with nature, a relationship characterised by 'the unleashing of an unrestrained and omnivorous ego upon the planet, a ravenous, hubristic and narcissistic self-driven by an illusion of its own complete agency and omnipotence' (Carney 2013: 219). The 'stylistic strangeness' of the play, from the jumbled and jangling opening soliloquy to the surreal parallel fairy narratives offers an incomprehensible **Other** as an 'essential affront to this ego' (Carney 2013: 219). When this psychoanalytical id, this terrifying, incomprehensible Other 'lashes back at humanity now, it is so slighted and damaged by our massive neglect that it destroys us utterly. No healthy relationship to the unconscious, the Skriker's world of faerie, is possible in this play' (Carney 2013: 220).

Carney's worry is that the play's apocalyptic depiction of our condition heralds the potential end of the tragic in a postmodern world, 'where nature has been extinguished and therefore regeneration through violence, sacrifice and submission is no longer possible' (Carney 2013: 220). But such confrontation of absolute loss without redemption would be the ultimate development of the genre in such a world. Churchill's play seems to offer just such a confrontation.

SARAH KANE, *BLASTED* (1995)

The shocking content of *Blasted* provoked a storm of indignation in the British press when it was first performed, but Kane's play has since established itself as a major piece of dramatic writing. In particular, *Blasted* demonstrated the enduring power of elements of classical tragedy in contemporary theatre. Indeed, the hostility with which the play was received can be seen as symptomatic of a postmodern culture wishing to deny the possibility of tragedy, an idea refuted by the power of Kane's work (Carney 2013: 266).

The play has two distinct parts. In the first, two ex-lovers, Cate and Ian, are in a luxurious hotel room in Leeds. Ian is a tabloid journalist, but it also seems as if he has been a killer for the security services or some other shadowy organisation (Kane 2001a: 29–30). He carries a gun in fear that his life is in danger from his former employers. Ian drinks heavily throughout the first half, and says he has not long to live: he has lung cancer (11) and cirrhosis of the liver. He is foul-mouthed, racist and alternately aggressive and pleadingly affectionate to Cate, with whom he wants to have sex. Ian has provided the symbols of a conventional romantic encounter, flowers and champagne. Cate is 24 years younger than the 45-year-old Ian (3). She still has some affection for him. She has come to spend the night because she was worried about him (4). Cate suffers from occasional blackouts. During one of these blackouts he '*simulates sex*' with her (35, stage direction) holding the gun to her head. She refuses full sex with him. The second scene takes place the following morning. Ian has raped Cate during the night.

So far the play has appeared an example of social realist theatre, albeit of a very sexually explicit kind. In the second scene Cate, having shown some tenderness towards him performs oral sex on Ian and bites him, perhaps in revenge. But the play suddenly takes a very different turn. While Cate is in the bath a foreign soldier enters and eats their breakfasts at gunpoint. Then a mortar bomb hits the hotel, blowing a hole in the wall (39). In the third scene, following the blast, the soldier boasts of the atrocities he has committed and tells of how the woman he loved, Col, was raped and mutilated, by the enemy. The soldier then rapes Ian, holding his gun at his head as Ian had done earlier to Cate (who has meanwhile escaped through the bathroom window). He sucks Ian's eyes out, as he says was also done to Col. At the beginning of the fourth scene the soldier has shot himself. Cate returns with a baby that a distressed woman has given her to look after, but it dies. In the final scene Cate buries the baby in the floor marking the grave with a cross and the remains of the flowers. She prays for the dead child and leaves Ian alone. During a wordless sequence Ian is left alone and in torment, performing basic human actions as time passes, the light coming and going (59–60). In his desperate hunger he finally eats the baby (a visual 'expression of his utter nihilism and despair'; Saunders 2002: 66) and climbs into its grave with the remains, with just his head visible above the floor. He dies, rain falling on him through the roof. Cate returns with gin and food. Ian has somehow survived death. She feeds him, and sits apart from him. But he says 'thank you' (61) as the rain falls and the play ends. The stage directions indicate that

Scene Two is set on a summer morning (24), Scene Four in the autumn (50) and Scene Five in the winter (57). The form of the play expresses its content: extreme violence, as happens in war, disorientates, confuses and changes people's fundamental perceptions of themselves and the world in an instant.

Blasted was written during the brutal wars in the Balkans which followed the break-up of Yugoslavia in the 1990s. As she wrote the play, Kane found herself reflecting on the terrible suffering she saw on television while she was just:

> writing this ridiculous play about two people in a room ... So I thought what could possibly be the connection between a common rape in a Leeds hotel and what's happening in Bosnia? And suddenly the penny dropped and I thought of course it's obvious, one is the seed and the other is the tree ... The seeds of full-scale war can always be found in peace-time civilisation.
>
> (cited in Saunders 2002: 39)

The connection between the soldier's rape of Ian and Ian's rape of Cate is clearly signalled by the repetition of the same image ('the soldier is a kind of personification of Ian's psyche'; Kane in Saunders 2002: 46). The damaged and diseased masculinity which Ian embodies in the first two scenes is of a piece with the sadistic cruelty of the soldier in the next two; Ian even chuckles that the soldier is 'worse than me' soon after they meet (40). Kane, who was influenced by the 'aggro effect' of Edward Bond (see above, p. 146), believed that extreme, violent actions on stage can have an impact on the audience so that 'we might be able to change our future, because experience engraves lessons on our hearts through suffering, whereas speculation leaves us untouched ... '. If an audience can 'commit to memory events never experienced – in order to avoid them happening' (cited in Saunders 2002: 22), then the powerful emotions evoked by such scenes might enable them to make the connections between the attitudes and beliefs they possess or encounter in their own lives and the violent manifestation of those same attitudes and beliefs elsewhere. In a radio interview in 2000 not long after she died Edward Bond said that Kane:

was able to penetrate very deeply what happens inside everybody ... If you let the outside world into yourself that is a chaotic and dramatic process and people don't like it ... Chaos is dangerous for us but we have to go into chaos to find ourselves.

(cited in Saunders 2002: 25)

There is a kind of **catharsis** at work here, and a possibility of redemption.

The images of Kane's play directly address subconscious and dark fears: of the foreign, of the latent violence just below the surface of our society. At the end of the play there stands the image of Ian's bloody head being cleansed by the rain. He dies, but is resurrected and fed by Cate. Finally he says 'thank you' to her. Kane said that *King Lear* was an important influence on her when writing the play (Saunders 2002: 58ff.) (hence, for example, the blinding of Ian, as with Gloucester in Shakespeare's tragedy, 3.7.66ff.). As in Elizabethan and Jacobean tragedy lust and bloody revenge (see above, p. 48) are central motive forces, but as in *King Lear* (and Bond's *Lear*) there is the also the reduction of the tyrant to the state of utter wretchedness which will induce pity in us. At the very end of the play both he and we can see Ian's common humanity and he finds some redemption: albeit in an infernal afterlife whose existence he denied (55). For all his vileness, Ian is honest and open about himself and his desires. There remains some possibility of goodness in him. But like Racine's Phèdre there will be no end to suffering even in death (see above, p. 90).

Elaine Aston writes that *Blasted* is a critique of a society where attempts to love and be loved back are blocked and corrupted by a misogynist masculinity which is pervasive in the play and beyond (Aston 2010: 24–25). Sean Carney also denies the straightforward possibility of love in the play. What he calls the 'broken' form of *Blasted* is a depiction of an incoherent, contradictory postmodern society where there are no wider narratives drawn from religion or the promise of human progress to make sense of human life any more (Carney 2013: 267). The huge scope and tragic vision of the play addresses the nature of the worst cruelties of human life: in Bosnia in 1992, in Syria at the time at which this book was written. The dramatist Rebecca

Pritchard is clear that the play 'is making connections between very intimate, personal perspectives and wider political reality … challenging an audience to deconstruct the values of their society as represented on stage, rather than merely asking them to empathise' (cited in Saunders 2002: 10). Terry Eagleton finds it distinctive of tragedy that in openly confronting the worst of human vulnerability and suffering we see a way forward (Eagleton 2008: 345).

FURTHER READING

Carney (2013) covers a broad range of contemporary English tragedy and develops a compelling argument about the relationship of these plays to modernism. Gritzner (2015) shows how Adorno's ideas are particularly useful in understanding British tragedy today. Other important tragedies include *Saved* (Bond 1990) *The Woman* (Bond 1987b) – which develops out of Greek tragedy – and *Bingo* (Bond 1987a), which imagines Shakespeare's death. Billingham (2013) is a good contemporary introduction to Bond, with Spencer (1992) also very useful. Plays by Howard Barker where he develops his Theatre of Catastrophe beyond Victory include *The Europeans* (Barker 2006a), *Hated Nightfall* (Barker 2009) and *Gertrude* (2006b), Barker's take on *Hamlet*. Rabey (1989) is probably still the best introduction to Barker. Useful collections on Barker include Gritzner and Rabey (2006) and Brown (2011). For *Angels in America*, Geis and Kruger (1997) bring together a wide-ranging collection of essays. Other Caryl Churchill plays to consider include *Top Girls* (Churchill 1982), *Far Away* (Churchill 2008a), *A Number* (Churchill 2008b) and her version of Seneca's *Thyestes* (Churchill 1998b). Aston and Diamond (2009) is a good place to start exploring Churchill criticism. Luckhurst (2014) is an excellent critical introduction to her work. Sarah Kane's *Cleansed* (Kane 2001b) is perhaps her other major tragedy, but *Phaedra's Love* (Kane 2001c) takes on Seneca's and Racine's tragedies. Saunders (2002) is a major study of Kane and de Vos and Saunders (2010) a collection of essays putting her work in context. Fernie (2007) addresses Lacan as an interpreter of tragedy most directly.

CONCLUSION

In 2015 a new version of the oldest tragedy, Aeschylus' *Oresteia* (see above, p. 9) was a surprising hit in the West End of London. Tragedy continues to draw audiences all over the world – indeed, the current international interest in producing Greek tragedy is 'completely unprecedented in scope and scale' (Hall 2010: 329). The first act of the 2015 *Oresteia* portrayed action that is only mentioned by the Chorus in Aeschylus' original (Aeschylus 2003: 52–3): the sacrifice by Agamemnon of his daughter Iphigenia, in fulfilment of prophecy, in order to obtain favourable winds so that the Greek fleet may attack Troy. Yet the setting of the play was firmly in the twenty-first century. In a heart-breaking scene, Iphigenia dies on stage in her father's arms, innocently taking the drugs (meticulously listed) which are used in euthanasia (Aeschylus 2015: 58). Agamemnon's religious faith was shown to be the reason why he agreed to this terrible sacrifice, but the play did not present this faith as archaic superstition leading to brutality. Faith here is one other way of trying to find meaning and purpose in a violent, conflicted world: 'not that there isn't meaning, there is, of course, it's just extremely hard to come by – with any sort of certainty', as the prophet Calchas puts it in the play's first speech (15). With archetypical tragic insight Agamemnon rejects the easy moral subjectivism which claims that doing the right thing is doing what feels right (52).

The French philosopher Jacques Derrida declared that tragedy is 'religion without religion' (cited in Fernie 2007: 34). Tragedy is the attempt to make art which transcends death, suffering and injustice by painfully insisting on our common frailty and on the brevity of our shared life. This transcendence is not necessarily spiritual, although it is clear that religious faith continues to play a powerful role in the world in the twenty-first century. Tragedy transcends the material conditions of life in order to come to terms in some effective way with those conditions. The power of what Adorno called 'instrumental reason' to strip 'enchantment' and ultimately human fellow-feeling from the world (see above, p. 152) is still resisted by art, and by tragedy in particular. New forms of this ancient art are evolving now, and will continue in the future to strive for some kind of transcendence of death, suffering and injustice, whatever dread crises remain waiting for us.

GLOSSARY

Anagnorisis: 'Tragic recognition': when a tragic protagonist realises the consequences of their irreparable error and their own culpability.

Catastrophe: Originally, the last part of a classical tragedy following the messenger's speech when disaster has struck the protagonist.

Catharsis: Generally, the emotional release on the part of the audience in response to the tragedy's climax, often with the idea that there is some kind of emotional benefit gained from the experience through expending powerful feelings. The term originates with Aristotle but there is some dispute about what he meant by the term (see above, p. 16)

Dramatic Irony: When the audience are aware of important information of which characters on stage are ignorant. It functions to intensify the emotional response of the spectators.

Enlightenment: The intellectual movement in the late seventeenth and eighteenth centuries which saw science and rationalism deliver great advances in technology. Denying the authority of tradition or unsubstantiated belief it insisted upon evidence and reason as the only grounds for knowledge in all areas of human activity.

Epic Theatre: A twentieth-century theatrical form which sought make its audience focus on the political and social reasons for action through various techniques, including emotional distancing, metatheatrical effects and the fragmentation of narratives and time schemes.

Existentialism: A school of philosophy originating in the nineteenth century, but most prevalent in the mid-twentieth, which regards humans as self-creating beings in an alien universe without larger purpose, who freely and authentically choose to endow themselves with qualities through their own actions, certain of their own mortality.

Hamartia: For Aristotle, the irreparable error of judgement committed by the protagonist which leads to the tragic outcome.

Hubris: Originally meaning 'harm' or 'insult', the Greek word has come to mean the excessive pride of the classical tragic protagonist which leads the gods bringing them down in retribution: *nemesis*.

Ideology: In this context, the stories a culture or society tells about itself which make its institutions, practices and values seem 'natural'. Originating in Marxist philosophy, in this sense of the term these narratives and explanations mask the contradictions of that society's way of life, particularly with regard to exploitation and social injustice.

Machiavel: A cunning, duplicitous and self-serving villain in early-modern tragedy (after the Italian political philosopher Niccolò Machiavelli (1469–1527).

Melodrama: A nineteenth-century popular theatrical form, often spectacular which aimed to evoked sentiment and presented a conventional moralism, with vice rewarded and virtue punished.

Metaphysics: Technically, the branch of philosophy which deals with what exists and what we can know. The term can be used negatively to dismiss abstract speculations which attempt to explain the world with reference to theoretical systems without grounding in material reality.

Metatheatre: Theatre which foregrounds itself as theatre, explicitly acknowledging its own fictional status to the audience.

Modernism: A late-nineteenth- and twentieth-century artistic movement responding to the conditions of industrialisation, urbanisation and loss of faith in God. Modernist thought tends to finds explanation for human activity in deep structures, such as in psychological, economic and sociological or anthropological factors. Modernist art seeks to break with traditional forms and reject single perspectives; it is often fragmented, introverted and imbued with a sense of crisis. But it can also celebrate the liberations of modern, technological urban existence.

Naturalism: In this context, theatre which attempts to depict 'real life' proceeding on stage as it apparently does for us, with everything explicable by natural causes.

Neoclassicism: From the seventeenth century onwards, a conscious attempt to imitate what were claimed to be the formal constraints of Greek and Roman art; in the theatre, adhering to the unities and observing 'decorum' in not mixing the comic and tragic or low-born with high-born characters.

Other: Generally, in critical theory, that which is totally different from the individual self constituted as a **subject**. Often alien and unknowable, in some cases threatening or hostile, it can also be the negative grounds against which individual subjectivity and even ethics are formed and created.

***Peripeteia*:** The moment in the tragedy when characters' expectations are overturned and a disastrous ending is shown to be inevitable.

Postmodernism: A wide-ranging late-twentieth-century and early-twenty-first century cultural phenomenon. Among its ideas can be found a rejection of 'grand narratives' (Christianity, Marxism, science) which give an explanatory force to human history. There is generally a denial of, or at least extreme scepticism about objective truth, and human cultures are seen to consist of competing narratives or 'discourses' whose credibility is a function of power, not veracity. The idea that much that we take as unified and stable (including our sense of ourselves as individuals) is actually a confected 'construction' based on larger social forces is also a feature of postmodern thought. Postmodern art can feature parody and pastiche, denying the possibility of genuine creative originality. It is generally relativist, refusing to ascribe more value to one artefact or art form than another, and denying any superiority of 'high' over 'popular' culture.

Protagonist: Meaning 'first actor' in Greek, the main character in a tragedy whose fall is the subject of the play.

Providence: The Christian belief that God is overseeing human life to ensure that the good are rewarded and the bad are punished, in this life and beyond.

Psychoanalysis: A school of thought whose original main proponent was Sigmund Freud, seeking to understand the human mind and behaviour through exploring the region which is not available to our normal self-awareness, the subconscious. The recovery of repressed feelings and desires in the earliest days of life and the exploration of family ties and emotions are an important aspect of its procedures.

Rhetoric: The crafting of language to persuade or impress, through patterning of its features or through manipulation of meanings in different ways. Learning to practise its techniques was an important part of classical and early-modern education.

Romanticism: An artistic and cultural movement in the late eighteenth and early nineteenth centuries which stressed the primacy of the emotions over reason, and the power of art and the individual imagination. Nature was a site of beauty and awe, not a raw material to be tamed and exploited. Politically romanticism often resisted established hierarchies and could be democratic in sympathy.

Soliloquy: A speech delivered by a character to the audience alone on stage.

Subject, Subjectivity: The term 'subject' in critical theory means an apparently individual consciousness which thinks itself as unified and autonomous, but is in fact constructed by language ('subject' in the grammatical sense) and by social political forces ('subject' in the political sense), which also act through language.

Unities: In neoclassical theory, the rule that a play must only have a single location (the unity of time) and a single plot (the unity of action) Its action must also be contained within a single day (the unity of time). These were not in fact stipulations of Aristotle, but in their prescriptive form dates from Ludovico Castelvetro's 1570 commentary on Aristotle's *Poetics*.

REFERENCES

Dates of first performance of plays are given in square brackets if they are different from the date of the publication cited.

Aeschylus (2003), *Agamemnon, The Libation Bearers* and *The Eumenides* [458 BCE], in *The Complete Aeschylus*, Vol. 1, trans. Peter Burian and Alan Shapiro (New York: Oxford University Press).

—— (2015), *Oresteia: A New Adaptation by Robert Icke* (London: Oberon Books).

Ahuja, Chaman (1984), *Tragedy, Modern Temper and O'Neill* (Delhi: Macmillan India).

Allan, Sean (1996), *The Plays of Heinrich von Kleist: Ideals and Illusions* (Cambridge: Cambridge University Press).

Amich, Candice (2007), 'Bringing the Global Home: The Commitment of Caryl Churchill's *The Skriker*', *Modern Drama* 50 (3) 394–413.

Anderson, Reed (1984), *Federico Garcia Lorca* (London: Methuen).

Aristophanes (1964), *The Frogs* [422 BCE], in *'The Wasps', 'The Poet and the Women' and 'The Frogs'*, trans. David Barrett (Harmondsworth: Penguin Books).

Aristotle (2013), *Poetics* [*c.* 340 BCE], trans. Anthony Kenny (Oxford: Oxford University Press).

Aston, Elaine and Elin Diamond (eds) (2009), *The Cambridge Companion to Caryl Churchill* (Cambridge: Cambridge University Press).

—— (2010), 'Reviewing the Fabric of *Blasted*', in Laurens de Vos and Graham Saunders (eds) *Sarah Kane in Context* (Manchester: Manchester University Press), 13–27.

Barker, Howard (1990), *Victory* [1983], in *Collected Plays*, Vol. 1 (London: John Calder), 133–95.

—— (1997), *Arguments for a Theatre*, 3rd edn (Manchester: Manchester University Press).

—— (2006a), *The Europeans* [1990], in *Plays One* (London: Oberon Books).

—— (2006b), *Gertrude* [2002], in *Plays Two* (London: Oberon Books).

—— (2009), *Hated Nightfall* [1994], in *Plays Five* (London: Oberon Books).

Beckett, Samuel (1956), *Waiting for Godot* [1953] (London: Faber and Faber).

—— (1958), *Endgame* and *Act Without Words* [1957] (New York: The Grove Press).

—— (2006), *The Complete Dramatic Works of Samuel Beckett* (London: Faber and Faber).

—— (2009), *Endgame* [1957] (London: Faber and Faber).

Behn, Aphra (2006), *Abdelazar* [1676], in Maureen Duffy (ed.) *Behn: Five Plays* (London: Bloomsbury), 379–475.

Belsey, Catherine (1985), *The Subject of Tragedy: Identity and Difference in Renaissance Drama* (London: Routledge).

—— (2007), *Why Shakespeare?* (Basingstoke and New York: Palgrave Macmillan).

Benjamin, Walter (1999), 'Theses on the Philosophy of History' [1940], in *Illuminations*, ed. Hannah Arendt, trans. Harry Zorn (London: Pimlico).

Bertens, Hans (2001), *Literary Theory: The Basics* (London: Routledge).

Bigsby, Christopher (2010), *The Cambridge Companion to Arthur Miller* (Cambridge: Cambridge University Press).

Billingham, Peter (2013), *Edward Bond: A Critical Study* (Basingstoke: Palgrave Macmillan).

Bloom, Harold (2003), *'Hamlet': Poem Unlimited* (Edinburgh: Canongate).

Blundell, Sue (1995), *Women in Ancient Greece* (London: The British Museum Press).

Bogard, Travis (1988), *Contour in Time: The Plays of Eugene O'Neill* (New York: Oxford University Press).

Bond, Edward (1983), *Lear* [1971] (London: Methuen).

—— (1987a), *Bingo* [1973], in *Plays: Three* (London: Methuen).

—— (1987b), *The Woman* [1979], in *Plays: Three* (London: Methuen).

—— (1990), *Saved* [1965], in *Plays: One* (London: Methuen).

—— (2013) 'Notes to Young Writers', in *The Activist Papers* [1976], in *Plays: Four* (London: Methuen).

Boyle, A. J. (1997), *Tragic Seneca: An Essay in the Theatrical Tradition* (London and New York: Routledge).

—— (2006), *Roman Tragedy* (London and New York: Routledge).

Bradley, A. C. (1991), *Shakespearean Tragedy* [1904] (London: Penguin Books).

Brecht, Bertolt (1983), *Mother Courage and her Children* [1941], trans. John Willett (London: Methuen).

—— (1996), *The Life of Galileo* [1940], trans. John Willett (London: Methuen).

—— (2015), *Brecht on Theatre*, ed. Marc Silberman, Steve Giles and Tom Kuhn, 3rd edn (London: Bloomsbury).

Brown, Mark (ed.) (2011), *Howard Barker Interviews 1980–2010: Conversations in Catastrophe* (Bristol: Intellect).

Büchner, Georg (2012), *Woyzeck* [1836], trans. Henry J. Schmidt, in Matthew Wilson Smith (ed.) *Georg Büchner: The Major Works* (New York and London: W. W. Norton & Co.), 133–69.

Canfield, J. Douglas (1989), *Word as Bond in English Literature from the Middle Ages to the Restoration* (Philadelphia: University of Pennsylvania Press).

—— (2000), *Heroes and States: On the Ideology of Restoration Tragedy* (Lexington: University of Kentucky Press).

Carney, Sean (2013), *The Politics and Poetics of Contemporary English Tragedy* (Toronto: University of Toronto Press).

Carter, D. M. (2007), *The Politics of Greek Tragedy* (Exeter: Bristol Phoenix Press).

Chekhov, Anton (1988a), *The Cherry Orchard* [1904], trans. Michael Frayn, in *Plays* (London: Methuen).

—— (1988b), *The Seagull* [1896], trans. Michael Frayn, in *Plays* (London: Methuen).

—— (1988c), *Uncle Vanya* [1889], trans. Michael Frayn, in *Plays* (London: Methuen).

Churchill, Caryl (1982), *Top Girls* (London: Methuen).

—— (1998a), *The Skriker* [1994], in *Plays: 3* (London: Nick Hern Books).

—— (1998b), *Thyestes* [1994], in *Plays: 3* (London: Nick Hern Books).

—— (2008a), *Far Away* [2000], in *Plays: 4* (London: Nick Hern Books).

—— (2008b), *A Number* [2002], in *Plays: 4* (London: Nick Hern Books).

Coleman, David (2010), *John Webster, Renaissance Dramatist* (Edinburgh: Edinburgh University Press).

Corneille, Pierre (2013), *Cinna* [1640], in *Four French Plays*, trans. John Edmunds (London: Penguin Books).

Cox, Jeffrey N. (1987), *In the Shadows of Romance: Romantic Tragic Drama in Germany, England and France* (Athens, OH: Ohio University Press).

Critchley, Simon (2008), 'I Want to Die, I Hate My Life: Phaedra's Malaise', in Rita Felski (ed.) *Rethinking Tragedy* (Baltimore: The John Hopkins University Press), 170–95.

Csapo, E. (2007), 'The Men who Built the Theatres', in P. Wilson (ed.) *The Greek Theatre and Festivals. Documentary Studies* (Oxford: Oxford University Press), 87–121.

Delgado, Maria M. (2008), *Federico Garcia Lorca* (London: Routledge).

Descartes, René (2015), *The Passions of the Soul* [1649], trans. Jonathan Bennett, available at www.earlymoderntexts.com/assets/pdfs/descartes1649.pdf (accessed 25 May 2015).

Diamond, Elin (2014), 'Churchill's Tragic Materialism: or, Imagining a Posthuman Tragedy', *PMLA* 129 (4) 751–60.

Dillon, Janette (2007), *The Cambridge Introduction to Shakespeare's Tragedies* (Cambridge: Cambridge University Press).

Dollimore, Jonathan (1984), *Radical Tragedy: Religion, Ideology and Power in the Drama of Shakespeare and his Contemporaries* (Brighton: Harvester Press).

Dryden, John (1986), *All for Love, or the World Well Lost* [1677], ed. N. J. Andrew (London: A&C Black).

Eagleton, Terry (2003), *Sweet Violence: The Idea of the Tragic* (Oxford: Blackwell).

—— (2008), 'Commentary', in Rita Felski (ed.) *Rethinking Tragedy* (Baltimore: The John Hopkins University Press), 337–46.

Easterling, P. E. (1997a), 'Form and performance', in P. E. Easterling (ed.) *The Cambridge Companion to Greek Tragedy* (Cambridge: Cambridge University Press), 151–77.

—— (ed.) (1997b), *The Cambridge Companion to Greek Tragedy* (Cambridge: Cambridge University Press).

Eliot, T. S. (1999), 'Four Elizabethan Dramatists' [1924], in *Selected Essays* (London: Faber and Faber).

Ellis-Fermor, Una (1945), *The Frontiers of Drama* (London: Methuen).

Euripides (1997), *Medea* [431 BCE], in *'Medea' and Other Plays*, trans. James Morwood (Oxford: Oxford University Press).

—— (2009), *Bacchae* [405 BCE], in *The Complete Euripides*, Vol. 4, trans. Reginald Gibbons and Charles Segal (New York: Oxford University Press), 243–301.

Fernie, Ewan (2002), *Shame in Shakespeare* (London and New York: Routledge).

—— (2007), 'Hardcore Tragedy', in Sarah Annes Brown and Catherine Silverstone (eds) *Tragedy in Transition* (Oxford: Blackwell), 34–57.

Freud, Sigmund (1953), *The Interpretation of Dreams* [1900], in *The Complete Psychoanalytical Works of Sigmund Freud*, trans. James Strachey, Vol. 4 (London: The Hogarth Press).

Friel, Brian (1996), *Translations* [1981], in *Brian Friel: Plays 1* (London: Faber and Faber).

Gagné, Renaud and Marianne Govers Hopman (2013), 'Introduction: The Chorus in the Middle', in Renaud Gagné and Marianne Govers Hopman (eds) *Choral Mediations in Greek Tragedy* (Cambridge: Cambridge University Press).

Garner, Stanton B. (1997), '*Angels in America*: The Millennium and Postmodern Memory', in Deborah R. Geis and Steven F. Kruger (eds) *Approaching the Millennium: Essays on 'Angels in America'* (Ann Arbor: University of Michigan Press).

Geis, Deborah R., and Steven F. Kruger (eds) (1997), *Approaching the Millennium: Essays on 'Angels in America'* (Ann Arbor: University of Michigan Press).

Geuss, Raymond (1999), 'Introduction', in Friedrich Nietzsche, *The Birth of Tragedy* [1872], ed. Raymond Geuss and Ronald Speirs, trans. Ronald Speirs (Cambridge: Cambridge University Press).

Gilman, Richard (1995), *Chekhov's Plays: An Opening into Eternity* (New Haven and London: Yale University Press).

Goldhill, Simon (1997a), 'The Audience of Athenian Tragedy', in P. E. Easterling (ed.) *The Cambridge Companion to Greek Tragedy* (Cambridge: Cambridge University Press), 54–68.

—— (1997b), 'Modern critical approaches to Greek Tragedy', in P. E. Easterling (ed.) *The Cambridge Companion to Greek Tragedy* (Cambridge: Cambridge University Press), 324–47.

—— (1986), *Reading Greek Tragedy* (Cambridge: Cambridge University Press).

—— (2004), *Love, Sex and Tragedy: Why Classics Matters* (London: John Murray).

—— (2007), *How to Stage Greek Tragedy Today* (Chicago and London: Chicago University Press).

Goldman, Lucien (1972), *Racine* [1952], trans. Alastair Hamilton (Cambridge: Rivers Press).

Gottlieb, Vera (2000), *The Cambridge Companion to Chekhov* (Cambridge: Cambridge University Press).

Grady, Hugh (2005), 'Tragedy and Materialist Thought', in Rebecca Bushnell (ed.) *A Companion to Tragedy* (Oxford: Blackwell).

—— (2014), 'The Modernity of Western Tragedy: Genealogy of a Developing Anachronism', *PMLA* 129 (4) 790–98.

Gritzner, Karoline (2008), '(Post)Modern Subjectivity and the New Expressionism: Howard Barker, Sarah Kane and Forced Entertainment', in *Contemporary Theatre Review* 18 (3) 328–40.

—— (2015), *Adorno and Modern Theatre: The Drama of the Damaged Self in Bond, Rudkin, Barker and Kane* (Basingstoke: Palgrave Macmillan).

Gurr, Andrew (2009a), *The Shakespearean Stage 1574–1642*, 4th edn (Cambridge: Cambridge University Press).

—— (2009b), 'Introduction', in Thomas Kyd, *The Spanish Tragedy*, ed. Andrew Gurr (London: Bloomsbury).

Hadfield, Andrew (2005), *Shakespeare and Republicanism* (Cambridge: Cambridge University Press).

Hall, Edith (2004), 'Introduction', in Edith Hall, Fiona Macintosh and Amanda Wrigley (eds) *Dionysus since 69: Greek Tragedy at the Dawn of the Third Millennium* (Oxford: Oxford University Press).

—— (2010), *Greek Tragedy: Suffering under the Sun* (Oxford: Oxford University Press).

—— (2014), 'To Fall from High or Low Estate? Tragedy and Social Class in Historical Perspective', *PMLA* 129 (4) 773–82.

Hawkes, Terence (1986), 'Telmah', in *That Shakespeherian Rag: Essays on a Critical Process* (London and New York: Methuen), 92–119.

Hazlitt, William (1857), 'On Shakespeare and Ben Jonson', in *Lectures on the English Comic Writers*, Vol. 4 (New York: Derby and Jackson), 32–67.

—— (1906), *Characters of Shakespeare's Plays* [1817] (London: J.M. Dent).

Herodotus (1972), *The Histories* [*c.* 430 BCE], trans. Aubrey de Sélincourt (Harmondsworth: Penguin Books).

Hopkins, Lisa (2008), *Christopher Marlowe, Renaissance Dramatist* (Edinburgh: Edinburgh University Press).

Howarth, William D. (1975), *Sublime and Grotesque: A Study of French Romantic Drama* (London: Harrap).

—— (1995), 'French Renaissance and Neo-Classical Theatre', in John Russell Brown (ed.), *The Oxford Illustrated History of Theatre* (Oxford: Oxford University Press), 220–51.

Hughes, Derek (1996), *English Drama 1660–1700* (Oxford: Clarendon Press).

Hugo, Victor (2004), *Four Plays*, ed. Claude Schumacher (London: Methuen).

Hume, David (1993), 'Of Tragedy' [1757], in *Selected Essays*, ed. Stephen Copley and Andrew Edgar (Oxford: Oxford University Press).

Ibsen, Henrik (1998a), *Hedda Gabler* [1890], trans. Jens Arup, in *Four Major Plays* (Oxford: Oxford University Press).

—— (1998b), *Ghosts* [1881], trans. James MacFarlane, in *Four Major Plays* (Oxford: Oxford University Press).

—— (1998c), *The Master Builder* [1892], trans. James MacFarlane, in *Four Major Plays* (Oxford: Oxford University Press).

—— (2009), *A Doll's House* [1987], trans. Michael Meyer (London: A&C Black).

James, Edward, and Gillian Jondorf (1994) *Racine: 'Phaedra'* (Cambridge: Cambridge University Press).

Jarvis, Simon (1998), *Adorno: A Critical Introduction* (Cambridge: Polity Press).

Jonson, Ben (1990), *Sejanus, His Fall* [1605], ed. Philip A. Ayers (Manchester: Manchester University Press).

Kane, Sarah (2001a), *Blasted* [1995], in *Complete Plays* (London: Bloomsbury).

—— (2001b), *Cleansed* [1998], in *Complete Plays* (London: Bloomsbury).

—— (2001c), *Phaedra's Love* [1996], in *Complete Plays* (London: Bloomsbury).

Kelsall, Malcolm (1969), 'Introduction', in Thomas Otway, *Venice Preserv'd* (London: Edward Arnold).

Kenny, Anthony (2013), 'Introduction', in Aristotle, *Poetics* [*c.* 340 BCE], trans. Anthony Kenny (Oxford: Oxford University Press).

Kerrigan, John (1996), *Revenge Tragedy: Aeschylus to Armageddon* (Oxford: Oxford University Press).

Kitto, H. D. F. (1966), *Greek Tragedy* (London: Methuen).

Kleist, Heinrich von (2002) *The Prince of Homburg* [1811], trans. Neil Bartlett with David Bryer (London: Oberon Books).

—— (2010) *The Prince of Homburg* [1811], trans. Dennis Kelly (London: Oberon Books).

Knox, Bernard M. W. (1983), 'The *Medea* of Euripides' [1977], in Erich Segal (ed.) *Oxford Readings in Greek Tragedy* (Oxford: Oxford University Press), 272–310.

Kott, Jan (1964), *Shakespeare Our Contemporary* (London: Methuen).

Kushner, Tony (1995), *Angels in America* (London: Nick Hern Books).

Kyd, Thomas (2009), *The Spanish Tragedy* [1588?], ed. Andrew Gurr (London: Bloomsbury).

Lacan, Jacques (1992), *The Ethics of Psychoanalysis 1959–60: The Seminar of Jacques Lacan*, Book 7, ed. Jacques-Alain Miller, trans. Dennis Porter (London: Routledge).

Lamb, Charles (2005), *The Theatre of Howard Barker* (London: Routledge).

Leavis, F. R. (1968), 'Viewpoints' [1936], in Bruce King (ed.) *Twentieth-Century Interpretations of 'All for Love': A Collection of Critical Essays* (Englewood Cliffs: Prentice-Hall), 105–8.

Leech, Clifford (1950), *Shakespeare's Tragedies* (London: Chatto and Windus).

Levin, Harry (1961), *Christopher Marlowe: The Overreacher* (London: Faber & Faber).

Loehlin, James N. (2010), *The Cambridge Introduction to Chekhov* (Cambridge: Cambridge University Press).

Lorca, Federico Garcia (1989), *Blood Wedding* [1933], trans. David Johnston (London: Hodder and Stoughton).

—— (1991a), *Yerma* [1934], trans. Carmen Zapata (Harmondsworth: Penguin Books).

—— (1991b), *The House of Barnarda Alba* [1936], trans. Carmen Zapata (Harmondsworth: Penguin Books).

Luckhurst, Mary (2014), *Caryl Churchill* (London: Routledge).

McEachern, Claire (2003), *The Cambridge Companion to Shakespeare's Tragedies* (Cambridge: Cambridge University Press).

McEvoy, Sean (2008), *Ben Jonson, Renaissance Dramatist* (Edinburgh: Edinburgh University Press).

—— (2016), *Theatrical Unrest: Ten Riots in the History of the Theatre 1601–2004* (London: Routledge).

MacFarlane, James (1994), *The Cambridge Companion to Ibsen* (Cambridge: Cambridge University Press).

Manheim, Michael (ed.) (1998), *The Cambridge Companion to Eugene O'Neill* (Cambridge: Cambridge University Press).

Marcus, Leah S. (2009), 'Introduction', in John Webster, *The Duchess of Malfi*, ed. Leah S. Marcus (London: Bloomsbury).

Marlowe, Christopher (1995a), *Doctor Faustus* [1588?], in *'Doctor Faustus' and other Plays*, ed. David Bevington and Eric Rasmussen (Oxford: Oxford University Press).

—— (1995b), *Tamburlaine The Great, Parts One and Two* [*c.* 1587–90], in *'Doctor Faustus' and other Plays*, ed. David Bevington and Eric Rasmussen (Oxford: Oxford University Press).

Middleton, Thomas (1996), *The Revenger's Tragedy* [1606], ed. R. A. Foakes (Manchester: Manchester University Press).

Middleton, Thomas and William Rowley (2007), *The Changeling* [1622], ed. Michael Neil (London: Methuen).

Miller, Arthur (1957), *Arthur Miller's Collected Plays* (New York: Viking Press).

—— (1961), *Death of a Salesman* [1949] (Harmondsworth: Penguin Books).

—— (2009), *All My Sons* [1947] (London: Penguin Books).

—— (2010), *A View from The Bridge* [1955], ed. Steve Marino (London: Methuen).

Mills, Sophie (2006), *Euripides' 'Bacchae'* (London: Bristol Classical Press).

Molière (2002), *Tartuffe* [1667], trans. Martin Sorrell (London: Nick Hern Books).

Murphy, Brenda (2014), *The Theatre of Tennessee Williams* (London: Methuen).

Nietzsche, Friedrich (1999), *The Birth of Tragedy* [1872], ed. Raymond Geuss and Ronald Speirs, trans. Ronald Speirs (Cambridge: Cambridge University Press).

Nuttall, A. D. (1996), *Why Does Tragedy Give Pleasure?* (Oxford: Clarendon Press).

O'Neill, Eugene (1991), *Long Day's Journey into Night* [1956] (London: Nick Hern Books).

—— (1992), *Mourning Becomes Electra* [1931] (London: Nick Hern Books).

Orr, John (1981), *Tragic Drama and Modern Society* (London: Macmillan).

Otway, Thomas (1969), *Venice Preserv'd* [1682], ed. Malcolm Kelsall (London: Edward Arnold).

Paolucci, Anne and Henry Paolucci (1962), 'Introduction', in *Hegel on Tragedy*, ed. Anne and Henry Paolucci (Westport: Greenwood Press).

Plato (1969), *Crito* [*c.* 390 BCE?], in *The Last Says of Socrates*, trans. Hugh Tredinnick (Harmondsworth: Penguin Books).

Poole, Adrian (2005), *Tragedy: A Very Short Introduction* (Oxford: Oxford University Press).

Rabey, David Ian (1989), *Howard Barker: Politics and Desire* (Basingstoke: Macmillan).

Racine (2013a), *Phaedra* [1677], in *Four French Plays*, trans. John Edmunds (London: Penguin Books).

—— (2013b), *Andromache* [1667], in *Four French Plays*, trans. John Edmunds (London: Penguin Books).

Reddick, John (1994), *Georg Büchner: The Shattered Whole* (Oxford: Oxford University Press). Extract in *Georg Büchner: The Major Works* (New York and London: W. W. Norton & Co.), 359–68.

Reiss, Timothy J. (2005), 'Using Tragedy against its Makers: Some African and Caribbean Instances, in Rebecca Bushnell (ed.) *A Companion to Tragedy* (Oxford: Blackwell).

Roberts, Adam (2000), *Fredric Jameson* (London: Routledge).

Roberts, David (2014), *Restoration Plays and Players* (Cambridge: Cambridge University Press).

Rousseau, Jean-Jacques (2008), *The Social Contract* [1762], ed. Christopher Betts (Oxford: Oxford University Press).

Ryan, Kiernan (2002), *Shakespeare*, 3rd edn (Basingstoke: Palgrave).

Saunders, Graham (2002), *'Love me or kill me': Sarah Kane and the Theatre of Extremes* (Manchester: Manchester University Press).

Savran, David (1997), 'Ambivalence, Utopia and a Queer Sort of Materialism: How *Angels in America* Reconstructs the Nation', in Deborah R. Geis and Steven F. Kruger (eds) *Approaching the Millennium: Essays on 'Angels in America'* (Ann Arbor: University of Michigan Press).

Schwartz, Alfred (1978), *From Büchner to Beckett: Dramatic Theory and the Modes of Tragic Drama* (Athens OH: Ohio University Press).

Segal, Erich (1983), (ed.) *Oxford Readings in Greek Tragedy* (Oxford: Oxford University Press).

Seneca, Lucius Annaeus (2010), *Phaedra* [*c.* 55 CE?], in *Six Tragedies*, trans. Emily Wilson (Oxford: Oxford University Press).

Shakespeare, William (1992), *The Tragedy of King Lear* [first published 1623] ed. Jay L. Halio (Cambridge: Cambridge University Press).

—— (2005), *The Oxford Shakespeare: The Complete Works*, ed. Stanley Wells and Gary Taylor, 2nd edn (Oxford: Oxford University Press).

—— (2006), *Hamlet* [1604–5], ed. Ann Thompson and Neil Taylor (London: Thomson Learning).

Shelley, Percy B. (2009), *The Cenci* [1819], in Zachary Leader and Michael O'Neill (eds) *Percy Bysshe Shelley: The Major Works* (Oxford: Oxford University Press).

Silberman, Marc, Steve Giles and Tom Kuhn (eds) (2015), *Brecht on Theatre* (London: Bloomsbury Methuen Drama).

Silk, M. S. (ed.) (1996), *Tragedy and the Tragic: Greek Theatre and Beyond* (Oxford: The Clarendon Press).

Silverstone, Catherine (2007), 'Afterword: Ending Tragedy', in Sarah Annes Brown and Catherine Silverstone (eds) *Tragedy in Transition* (Oxford: Blackwell), 277–86.

Smith, Emma and Garret A. Sullivan (2010), *The Cambridge Companion to English Renaissance Tragedy* (Cambridge: Cambridge University Press).

Sokol, B. J. (2008), *Shakespeare and Tolerance* (Cambridge: Cambridge University Press).

Sophocles (1982), *Antigone* [*c.* 442 BCE] and *Oedipus the King* [*c.* 430 BCE], in *The Three Theban Plays*, trans. Robert Fagles (London: Penguin Books).

Soyinka, Wole (1973), *The Bacchae of Euripides* (London: Methuen).

Spencer, Jenny S. (1992) *Dramatic Strategies in the Plays of Edward Bond* (Cambridge: Cambridge University Press).

Stanton, Edward F. (1978), *The Tragic Myth: Lorca and 'Cante Jondo'* (Lexington: University of Kentucky Press).

Steiner, George (1961), *The Death of Tragedy* (London: Faber and Faber).

—— (2008), '"Tragedy" Reconsidered', in Rita Felski (ed.) *Rethinking Tragedy* (Baltimore: The John Hopkins University Press), 29–44.

Stern, Robert (2013), *The Routledge Guidebook to Hegel's 'Phenomenology of Spirit'* (London and New York: Routledge).

Strindberg, August (2008a), *Miss Julie* [1888], in Michael Robinson (ed.) *'Miss Julie' and Other Plays* (Oxford: Oxford University Press).

—— (2008b), *The Dance of Death* [1900], in Michael Robinson (ed.) *'Miss Julie' and Other Plays* (Oxford: Oxford University Press).

Taplin, Oliver (1985), *Greek Tragedy in Action* (London: Routledge).

Tate, Nahum (1997), *King Lear* [1681], in Sandra Clark (ed.) *Shakespeare Made Fit: Restoration Adaptations of Shakespeare* (London: J.M. Dent).

Thomson, Peter (1997), *Brecht, Mother Courage and her Children* (Cambridge: Cambridge University Press).

Thomson, Peter and Glendyr Sacks (eds) (2010), *The Cambridge Companion to Brecht* (Cambridge: Cambridge Univesity Press).

Thucydides (1972), *The Peloponnesian War*, trans. Rex Warner (Harmondsworth: Penguin Books).

Tomlin, Liz (2006), 'A New Tremendous Aristocracy: Tragedy and the Meta-Tragic in Barker's Theatre of Catastrophe', in Caroline Gritzner and David Ian Rabey (eds) *Theatre of Catastrophe: New Essays on Howard Barker* (London: Oberon Books), 109–23.

Törnqvist, Egil (1998), 'O'Neill's Philosophical and Literary Paragons', in Michael Manheim (ed.) *The Cambridge Companion to Eugene O'Neill* (Cambridge: Cambridge University Press).

Van Hulle, Dirk (2015), *The New Cambridge Companion to Samuel Beckett* (Cambridge: Cambridge University Press).

Vernant, Jean-Pierre (1983), 'Ambiguity and Reversal: On the Enigmatic Structure of *Oedipus Rex*', in Erich Segal (ed.) *Oxford Readings in Greek Tragedy* (Oxford: Oxford University Press), 189–209.

—— (1988), *Myth and Tragedy in Ancient Greece* (New York: Zone).

de Vos, Laurens and Graham Saunders (eds) (2010), *Sarah Kane in Context* (Manchester: Manchester University Press).

Wallace, Jennifer (2007), *The Cambridge Introduction to Tragedy* (Cambridge: Cambridge University Press).

Webster, John (2009), *The Duchess of Malfi* [1613–14], ed. Leah S. Marcus (London: Bloomsbury).

Wheatley, Christopher J. (2000), 'Tragedy', in Deborah Payne Fisk (ed.), *The Cambridge Companion to English Restoration Theatre* (Cambridge: Cambridge University Press), 70–85.

Weiss, Katherine (2012), *The Plays of Samuel Beckett* (London: Methuen).

Wiles, David (2000), *Greek Theatre Performance: An Introduction* (Cambridge: Cambridge University Press).

Williams, Raymond (1979), *Modern Tragedy*, rev. edn (London: Verso).

Williams, Tennessee (2005), *A Streetcar Named Desire* [1947], ed. Patricia Hern (London: Methuen).

—— (2009a), *Cat on a Hot Tin Roof* [1954], (London: Penguin Books).

—— (2009b), *The Glass Menagerie* [1945], (London: Penguin Books).

Wilson, Richard (2000), '"Writ in blood": Marlowe and the New Historicists', in J.A. Downie and J.T. Parnell (eds), *Constructing Christopher Marlowe* (Cambridge: Cambridge University Press), 116–32.

Woodbridge, Linda (2010), *English Revenge Tragedy: Money, Resistance, Equality* (Cambridge: Cambridge University Press).

Zeitlin, Froma I. (1996), *Playing the Other: Gender and Society in Classical Greek Literature* (Chicago and London: University of Chicago Press).

INDEX

Taylor & Francis eBooks